WARSHIPS

Almost from the dawn of history man has been adept as a warrior on the seas—as Homer's famous *Odyssey* and the tale of Jason and the Argonauts attest. Propelled by a combination of sails and oars, the galley of antiquity reached its peak in the navies of Greece and Rome—the sleek trireme whose legendary swiftness in combat was owed to disciplined oarsmen. A thousand years passed, finding Venice and France, the leading naval powers of Renaissance Europe, still dedicated to the galley. Several centuries afterward, wood and sail, and even oarsmen, in the case of the fabled Spanish galleon, held sway as the main design features of the man-of-war in the Age of Exploration.

Indeed, almost up until the onset of the American Civil War—more than 50 years after Robert Fulton had built the steamship *Claremont* in 1807—the world's seagoing fighting ships had changed basically only in terms of size (and, of course, armament) in some 3,000 years of history. In the following pages, we attempt to document the modern revolution in the design of warships that has radically altered the nature of sea power in the past hundred years. Beginning with the introduction of steam and armor, the pace of innovation surges unremittingly forward into the present-day era of missiles and nuclear-powered propulsion. Because this story is truly international in scope, the reader will find color illustrations of vessels of many nations—each one representing a milestone in warship design.

This book is an adaptation
from an original work by H. T. Lenton

A
GROSSET
ALL-COLOR GUIDE

WARSHIPS

BY JACQUES SIMMONS

Illustrated by David A. Warner & Nigel W. Hearn

GROSSET & DUNLAP
A NATIONAL GENERAL COMPANY
Publishers • New York

THE GROSSET ALL-COLOR GUIDE SERIES
SUPERVISING EDITOR ... GEORG ZAPPLER
Board of Consultants

CONTENTS

1737011

INTRODUCTION

In the first half of the 19th century, the man-of-war, cruising under sail, her armament consisting of bristling broadsides of cannon, reigned supreme on the high seas. The biggest of the men-of-war was the 'ship-of-the-line.' Her broadside ranged up to several score cannon, arranged on three or more gundecks. Her mission, like that of the later battleship, comprised heavy action at sea and shore bombardment. She also played an instrumental role in the blockading of enemy ports. In short, the ship-of-the-line was the heaviest and most powerful warship of the days of sail, and her successor is the modern battleship.

The next most feared vessel—perhaps often more so because of her speed—was the 'frigate.' This class of sailing ship was typified by the famed *U.S.S. Constitution*. Faster than the ship-of-the-line, the frigate had a smaller displacement (tonnage); its two gundecks carried as few as 24 cannon or as many as 50. Smaller than the frigate, but performing related missions, was the 'corvette.' These two ships performed scouting, escort and raiding missions, not unlike their successors, the cruisers. Smaller still, and therefore more maneuverable at close quarters, were the 'sloop' and the 'gunboat.' (Men-of-war were further distinguished as 'brigs,' 'brigantines,' 'barks,' 'schooners,' 'clippers,' and so on, according to the number and placement of their masts, the way in which their sails were rigged, and the shape of their hulls—particularly the stem and stern.)

Sailing men-of-war carried most of their armament in fixed rows along the ship's side—an arrangement called 'the broadside.' The cannon fired solid shot (cannon balls) that was loaded at the muzzle after the powder bag or bags had first also been rammed down the muzzle into place. Such guns were generally truck-mounted, that is, on rollers. They were rolled forward, in the firing position, to protrude through gunwales or ports; on firing, the recoil force caused the cannon to return to the loading position. Their bores were smooth. By way of contrast, the bores of modern guns are rifled with grooves that give spin to the outgoing projectile. This spin acts to stabilize the flight of the projectile, as does the spin put on a forward pass by a quarterback. Rifled guns are more accurate than smooth-bore guns and have longer ranges.

The sailing frigate man-of-war was typified by the *U.S.S. Constitution* which sank the British ship *Java* during the War of 1812.

Beginning in the 19th century, steam engines were employed to propel vessels by means of paddle wheels. Mounted alongside the hull, the paddle wheel took up space, thereby reducing the number of cannon that could be carried in the broadside. Early steam engines were inefficient and required huge stores of coal on board ship. Boiler explosions and accidental fires were common. For these reasons, the early steam-and-sail man-of-war normally cruised under full sail, getting up steam only if the wind died or in maneuvering in combat. Then, however, the paddle wheel was exposed to enemy guns. This problem was finally solved with the introduction of screw propulsion, with the now invulnerable screw protected beneath the waterline at the ship's stern.

When shell—far more penetrating than shot, which was round rather than pointed—came into use, navies reacted by armoring warships with iron plate fixed to the wood hull. Most plate was situated above the waterline, causing topheaviness and vulnerability to capsizing; therefore, the upper gundecks had to be eliminated.

During the Civil War, the Union *Monitor* introduced the turret system of mounting guns. In the broadside arrangement, the whole ship had to be turned to train the guns on a moving target. But turrets did not readily lend themselves to use on sailing ships; the masts, rigging, and the raised decks at the

The British battleship *Agincourt* was completed in 1867.

The British mine counter-measure support ship *Abdiel* (1967).

stem and stern (the 'fo'c'sle' and the 'poop,' respectively), created obstructions limiting the rotating turret's arc of fire. But once steam could be used exclusively (which happened first in coast defense vessels that did not need the sail for long voyages), the deck was cleared for incorporation of the rotating turret. Thereafter, the warship no longer had to come about constantly to fire on a moving target; its turrets did the job. Eventually, steam was also harnessed to provide auxiliary power for hydraulic machinery that rotated the turret and elevated its guns, making heavier armament possible. In time, hull and superstructure design were modified to permit the mounting of turrets in echelon ('wedding-cake' style) on the centerline fore and aft, so that the guns could be fired axially (backward or forward) or rotated to fire to the side.

Then, while the armored warship was growing as impervious to injury as the armadillo inside its shell, torpedoes and mines were introduced to attack the more lightly armored portions of the hull below the waterline. But we are ahead of our story.

CAPITAL SHIPS

The British battleship *Warrior*

Although the American Civil War (1861–65) provided the setting for the first engagement between ironclad warships, the previous decade had seen both France and England incorporate armor plate and steam propulsion into the design of their largest warships (or *capital ships*). Britain's *Warrior* exemplifies contemporary naval thinking with respect to the use of steam; namely, that while the high speed given by steam was desirable in combat, the sail was still more trustworthy for seagoing voyages. Hence, the *Warrior,* whose keel was laid in 1859, had masts and rigging, as well as ten boilers generating 5,000 horsepower and yielding 14 knots (nautical miles per hour, a nautical mile being 800 feet longer than a standard land mile). With a narrow clipper stem, the *Warrior's* hull displaced over 9,000 tons (see 'displacement;' Glossary, p. 157). A belt of armor plate, $4\frac{1}{2}$ inches thick and secured on hull planks a foot-and-a-half thick, ran 213 feet along the sides, extending 6 feet below the waterline and 16 feet above. Although this belt covered the hull only partially, leaving the ends unprotected, bulkheads (walls) of iron were installed internally to shield machinery and ammunition magazines from shell penetrating the stem or stern. The *Warrior's* broadside included eight 110-pounder, breech-loading smooth-bore guns, as well as 28 muzzle-loading 68-pounders.

The Union Navy's revolutionary *Monitor*
When the Civil War began in 1861, the Confederate armies forced the abandonment of Union installations below the Mason-Dixon Line. Before retreating from the Norfolk Navy Yard at Portsmouth, Virginia, Union officers scuttled the steam-frigate *Merrimack* to prevent its falling into Southern hands. Soon the Union received alarming news: the *Merrimack* had been raised and was hurriedly being reconverted into an ironclad capable of decimating the wooden vessels with which the Union was enforcing its coastal blockade of Southern ports.

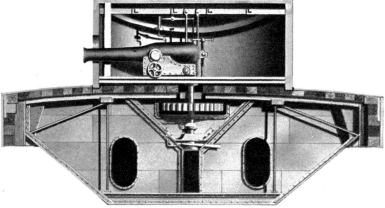

(*Above*) Cross-section of the American *Monitor* (1862) and (*below*) the Swedish monitor *John Ericsson* (1866).

These illustrations show the development of the breastwork monitor in the British Royal Navy from the low freeboard *Cyclops* of 1877 (*above*) to the *Dreadnought* of 1879 (*below*).

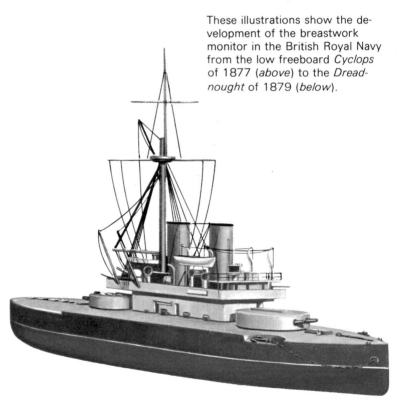

The North was desperate. The Union must have an iron-clad of its own to fend off the *Merrimack* and to protect its blockading ships. The Swedish engineer Ericsson undertook to build such a vessel for the Union within 100 days, the time within which Union intelligence reports suggested the *Merrimack* would be in action. Because of lack of time, Ericsson had to settle for a small ironclad with a shallow draft (see Glossary, p. 157). In fact, Ericsson's ideas were shortly to revolutionize naval design principles. He relied solely on steam propulsion; without rigging, he was able to arm his ironclad with a turret (mounting two muzzle-loading 11-inch guns) with a free 360° arc of fire. This ship, named the *Monitor,* was fitted with a raft-like armored breastwork that extended down over the shipshape hull and protected the waterline.

On March 8, 1862, the *Merrimack* (rechristened the *Virginia*) made its debut off Hampton Roads, sinking two Union vessels and scattering others. On coming out the next day, however, she found herself confronted by the strange-looking *Monitor.* Although the *Virginia* was far more heavily armed, she never defeated the little *Monitor* in their encounters.

The breastwork—monitor
The *Monitor's* strengths impressed the Confederacy as well as Great Britain. Thus, in the same year, 1862, British yards

laid down a pair of turret ships for the Confederate Navy. Since the Confederacy wanted seagoing vessels, neither rode as low in the water as Ericsson's original coast defense vessel. Rather, they showed six feet of freeboard (see Glossary); they also were fully rigged with sail and possessed a fo'c'sle (forecastle) and a poop deck to provide cabin space and to render the bow and stern more seaworthy. But the masts and rigging, like the fo'c'sle and poop, were incompatible with the turret mount, since the turret requires a flush, unobstructed deck in order to fire freely.

By 1867, too late for the Confederacy, British naval architects succeeded in producing their own *Monitor*-class vessel. The turrets were carried at each end of an armored breastwork on the main deck; elevated 10½ feet above the waterline, they commanded a clear field of fire. The British 'monitors' saw service as coast defense craft in the colonies, but steam was not yet reliable enough for ocean voyages and prevented wider adoption of the turret.

The central battery ship

The battleship was now evolving along two paths: on the one hand, the deep-draft, fully rigged, sea-going ship, carrying

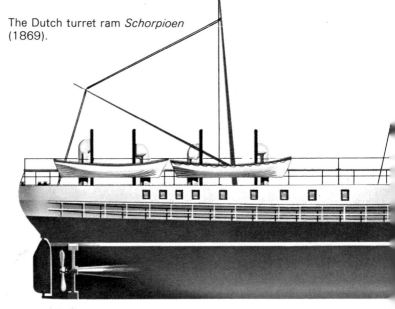

The Dutch turret ram *Schorpioen* (1869).

guns on the broadside; and on the other hand, the shallow-draft, unrigged, coast defense turret ship.

As guns grew larger, fewer could be carried broadside. Those that were carried were grouped amidships in a central battery. The armored belt—which did not cover the whole hull in the case of the *Warrior*—now stretched from end to end down to the waterline. Amidships, the belt was extended up to shield the central battery. To protect the gun positions against raking fire coming in over the stem and stern, athwartships armored bulkheads (see Glossary) were erected across the ends of the battery. The battery was meant not only to fire sideways but also forward and backward along the axis of the ship, over stem and stern. To provide axial fire, the central battery was elevated and the superstructure fore and aft of the battery was recessed.

The turret ram
In 1866, the Austro-Hungarian and Italian fleets, battling in coastal waters, gave prominence to the ram as a weapon. Thereafter, the threat of the ram bedevilled designers for years, until

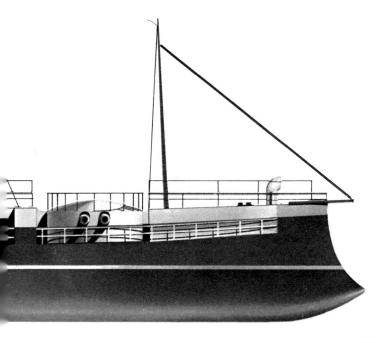

maneuvers demonstrated the difficulties inherent in ramming a ship on the move.

As an effective ram a ship had to have a small turning circle; this meant she had to be short and small. A single turret forward to keep the enemy under fire while closing the range was thought sufficient. The resulting turret ram emerged as a coast defense ship and was not rigged. For small navies, the turret ram was popular and many were built.

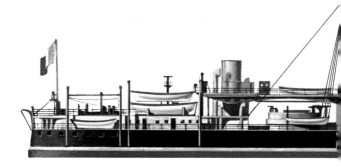

The masted turret ship

The advocates of the turret system pressed their claim in advance of their time. When applied to low-freeboard coast defense ships, there was no denying the advantage of the turret system. But it was a different matter — as already explained — when applied to sea-going ships of high freeboard with all the impedimenta associated with the full rig.

The weight of the turret prevented it from being carried high, and to reduce freeboard while maintaining a full spread of canvas was constructionally unsound — and so it proved. In 1866 the British Navy laid down the *Monarch*, which in essence was a central battery ship with the guns in two turrets carried a deck higher and freeboard amidships reduced to 14 feet. In the next year she was followed by the *Captain*, with the turrets wider spread and the superstructure angled to improve their arcs but with only 8½-foot freeboard amidships. Unfortunately, excess weights decreased the *Captain's* freeboard by a further two feet and in 1870, only six months after completion, she capsized and sank in heavy weather in the Bay of Biscay.

As a result of this tragedy the turret system suffered a temporary setback, but the British *Devastation*—laid down only a year after the *Captain*—heralded the abolition of masts and yards and the universal acceptance of the turret. An upward development of the breastwork monitor, the *Devastation* could stow 1,800 tons of coal and had a radius of 4,700 miles at 10 knots—a range that was more than adequate for the distances involved between coaling stations.

The Italian *Dandolo* of 1882 (*above*) and the British *Inflexible* of 1881 (*below*) were typical of the short-lived masted turret ship.

The mastless turret ship

In the last three decades of the 19th century, advances in ordnance greatly influenced the evolution of the battleship. Guns were steadily increasing in size. At first, these gains in firepower were translated not so much into the range over which projectiles could be fired as into the weight and destructive force of the projectile.

In the 1870's, Italy, fearing French naval build-ups in the

(*Above*) The open barbette ship *Royal Sovereign* (1892) and (*below*) the closed barbette vessel *Jauréguiberry* (1896).

Mediterranean and realizing she could not match the French ship for ship, decided to settle on fewer vessels of much greater firepower than those possessed by the French fleet. Brin, the Italian naval architect, first cast his battleship design around the use of guns weighing 50 tons, with bore-diameters of 15 inches (see Glossary), that could hurl a massive projectile

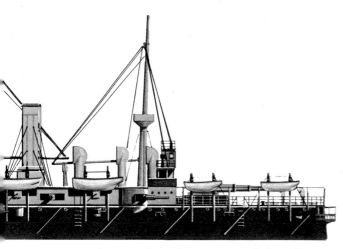

many times heavier than the 110-pound shot that comprised the heaviest armament of warships of the prior decade. Brin later stepped up his plans to include 100-ton, 17.7-inch guns.

The 17-inch diameter projectile of the period could weigh many hundreds of pounds, depending on the type of propellant available; and new, slow-burning powders, capable of propelling shells of increasing size at higher and higher muzzle velocities were now appearing from munitions makers. The armor necessary to stop such big shells was so thick that protection could be afforded only amidships. A central armored 'citadel' was therefore conceived, grouping boilers, machinery, and magazines, as well as turrets. The main deck was armored, as was the hull.

Laid down to such specifications in 1873, the Italian battleships *Dandolo* and *Duilio* could outrun most other battleships then in service, attaining speeds of 15 knots. Their muzzleloading ordnance proved cumbersome, however; the long gun barrels had to be loaded from outside the turrets. This fact contributed to a final shift by designers to breech-loaders.

The barbette ship

Heavy turrets are operated by hydraulic machinery or electric motors drawing power from the ship's hold. Hence, turret mounts were generally restricted to the level of the main deck. But fixed gun positions could readily be placed anywhere on the battleship. The so-called barbette gun position began as a fixed mount without armor. Thereafter, the difference between it and the turret became almost indistinguishable. First, bullet-proof shelters were erected at the rear of the station for the loading crew. Later, armored shielding was built around the front and sides to protect the entire gun crew — the gun protruding over the top of the shield or through an opening in it. Once battleship designers abandoned the concept of the central armored 'citadel' amidships, the main gun positions, both fore and aft, became separate armored stations. Heavy armor plate was added to the shield and the rear of the station was also plated in. At this point, the barbette resembled a sawed-off turret in appearance. The turret now meant the revolving armored structure, whereas the barbette implied a similar, but fixed, structure.

Meanwhile, offensive thinkers were introducing secondary batteries of medium-caliber guns to attack the unarmored ends

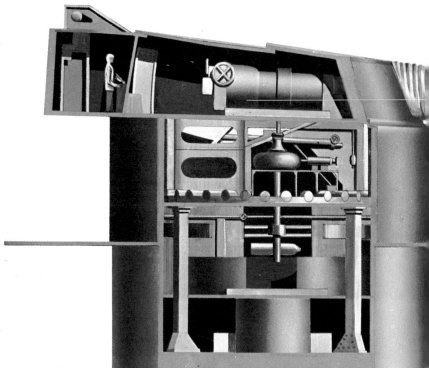

of rival warships. (Caliber is a measure of the gun's bore-diameter; a 50-caliber machine-gun, for example, has a bore-diameter of 50/100ths of an inch; in other words, it is the equivalent of a half-inch gun. A 40-millimeter gun falls between one and two inches. See Glossary.) This rapid adoption of medium-caliber, fast-firing weapons caused battleship designers to extend a thin armored belt around the bow and stern along the waterline.

For the battleship of the late 19th century, however, the chief nemesis became the torpedo boat—swift and maneuverable, able to close rapidly on its more ponderous victim. In the last two decades of the century, the very existence of the battleship was threatened by the torpedo. Defenders tried spreading anti-torpedo netting around the ship. They re-engineered the battleship's power plant to increase its speed and maneuverability. A tertiary battery of medium-caliber guns was installed on the superstructure amidships to drive off the torpedo

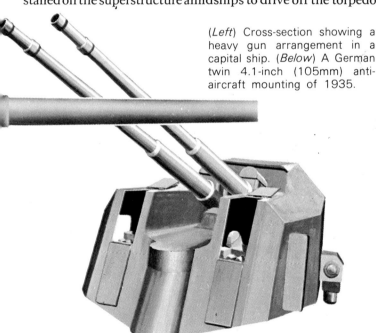

(*Left*) Cross-section showing a heavy gun arrangement in a capital ship. (*Below*) A German twin 4.1-inch (105mm) anti-aircraft mounting of 1935.

boats before they closed within torpedo range. Then, during World War I, the battleship's protagonists came up with some long-lasting innovations. First, they affixed to the hull a bulging, external anti-torpedo bulkhead. This ran along the waterline at the ship's side. More than likely a torpedo would rupture only this false 'bulge,' while the true hull remained intact. In addition, the hold's interior was compartmentalized thoroughly with bulkheads. Thus, by closing water-tight hatches, crew members could seal off behind bulkheads any part of the hold that shipped water as the result of a break in the hull. Although such steps diminished the threat of the torpedo, strategists nevertheless recognized that the close blockade of an enemy coast by capital units was henceforth ruled out.

Because the battleship had become so overcrowded with arms, the United States resorted to superimposing turrets in echelon (wedding-cake style) to save deck space. The *Kearsarge*-class battleship mounted twin 8-inch guns over twin 13-inch guns.

The dreadnought battleship
For years, the main guns of a battleship could be brought onto target only at short ranges, restricting fleets to close-quarters action. In the 1890's, improved optical rangefinding instruments were introduced. With these, the first salvo was fired, and then the margin by which the salvo missed — or bracketed

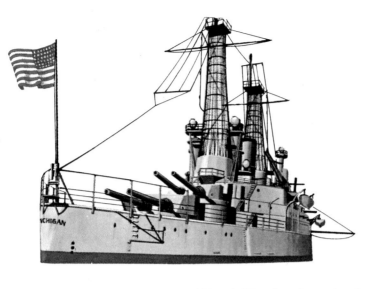

(*Above*) The American dreadnought battleship *Michigan*
(1910). (*Below*) The British prototype *Dreadnought* (1906).

—the target was measured through the new optical range-finder. The appropriate corrections were relayed to the gunners. Thus, salvo following after salvo, the guns were gradually zeroed in.

The first warship with enough main guns to exploit long-range gunnery fully was the famous British *Dreadnought,* whose salvos comprised ten 12-inchers twin-mounted in five turrets—two of them winged off the center line for axial fire (see page 13). The *Dreadnought* also carried a battery of anti-torpedo boat weapons. Her main propulsion was revolutionary for her day, consisting of steam turbines that gave her at least three knots advantage over existing battleships.

Because her designers foresaw long-range action, they greatly increased the thickness of the *Dreadnought's* deck armor. At close quarters, shells are fired along fairly flat trajectories (or paths). Shots fired at a far-away object must be given more lift in order to carry; hence, in striking, they plunge down from the sky rather than come in parallel to the water. Long-range action would bring shells down onto the decks.

The *Dreadnought* so completely outclassed existing battleships that other nations were forced to construct ships of equal speed and armament. The British had already enjoyed battleship supremacy before building the *Dreadnought* and

stimulating other navies to construct like ships. Britain recognized that by building the *Dreadnought* it would force a naval arms race, and, in effect, render its own already superior battleships obsolete. But Britain knew that similar designs were already under active consideration in other navies, and, rather than wait for others, the British took the initiative.

Indeed, Germany and Japan soon followed by building dreadnought battleships similar to the British design. American ships were also similar, but employed four center-line turrets, with the inner pair superimposed (see page 20). The United States' vessels had the same broadside as the others, and maneuvers proved that the sacrifice in axial fire—ahead and astern—was negligible. Later, therefore, the classic simplicity of the American arrangement was universally copied.

The dreadnought cruiser

After breaking new ground with the *Dreadnought,* the British Royal Navy did the same with armored cruisers. In the *Invincible* of 1906, the armored cruiser was expanded to accommodate eight 12-inch guns. The adoption of a steam-turbine power plant gave it speeds at least two knots faster than existing armored cruisers. Like the *Dreadnought,* the *Invincible* and cruisers patterned after her rendered obsolete older ships.

Just over a decade of battle-cruiser development separates the British prototype *Invincible* of 1906 (*below*) from the German *Hindenburg* of 1917 (*above*).

The *Invincible's* eight 12-inch guns were twin-mounted in four turrets—one forward, another aft and one each on the beam amidships to augment axial fire. In such a vessel, strategists recognized a capital ship with armament of battleship caliber, and yet a ship with greater mobility than the battleship. The prospect of employing the battle cruiser to form a high-speed, flanking wing of the battle fleet captured the contemporary naval imagination. To increase its speed while retaining its fire-power, more and more of the battle cruiser's armored protection was stripped away. Entering World War I, therefore, the battle cruiser's reputation as a swift, powerful warship perhaps capable of out-dueling the battleship itself was enormous. But at Jutland the myth was cruelly shattered, for there the British lost three of their glamorous new battle cruisers, and two of the losses were directly attributable to insufficient protective armor. The battle cruiser's extra speed had been secured at too high a price.

The battle cruiser's demise was further hastened by new technology in the power plant. Around the time of World War I the general naval changeover from coal-fired to oil-fired steam-turbine engines made possible battleships with speeds of 25 knots, overcoming the mobility advantage previously enjoyed by *Invincible*-class battle cruisers. Because comparatively swift yet fully armored battleships were now possible, the trend to the battle cruiser was halted. In its *Nevada*-class battleships, the United States reverted to an 'all-or-nothing' system of protection similar to the early turret and barbette ship, and the United States' lead was followed by other navies.

Battleships between the wars

After World War I, under the terms of the Washington Naval Treaty (1921), battleships were restricted to a displacement of no more than 35,000 tons; they were to carry guns no larger than 16 inches in bore diameter. At the time the treaty was signed, the American, British and Japanese navies had on their drawing boards plans for battleships of up to 50,000 tons. As a result of the treaty, none of these ships was built.

Following World War I, a new threat to the battleship loomed—attack from the air. It was not so much the bomber as the torpedo plane that posed the most serious challenge to the battleship's supremacy. Yet, while the battleship never

Bridge details of the British battle cruiser *Tiger* (1914).

Multiple gun turrets were a feature of ship construction between
the World Wars. (*Above*) Triple
turrets in the Italian battleship
Littorio (1940). (*Below*) The
quadruple turrets of the French
battle cruiser *Dunkerque* (1937).

claimed invulnerability to air and torpedo attack, it was not
quite a 'sitting duck,' as claimed by its scornful critics. By
further thickening its deck armor, as had already been done
once to shield against long-range plunging fire from naval guns,
some security against the dive-bomber was afforded. And the
steps taken to secure the waterline against the torpedo boat
were as effective against the torpedo plane. Furthermore, a
thick tertiary battery of anti-aircraft guns was, as we shall see,
added to the battleship's armament, while by traveling in
force with escort aircraft carriers the battleship gained the protection of interceptor planes. Between 1921 and 1935, Britain
and France, signatories of the Washington Treaty, each laid
down a pair of new capital ships, as did Germany, a non-
signatory.

The British ships, the *Nelson* and the *Rodney,* were interesting in that they placed their main armament of 16-inch guns in three triple turrets forward so that armored protection could be concentrated over a compact area. To meet air attack they were given a 6¼-inch thick steel deck, while the external anti-torpedo bulge (see page 20)—a successful war-time innovation—was replaced by an internal system of longitudinal bulkheads. The secondary anti-torpedo armament was placed in upperdeck turrets aft, and the tertiary armament now comprised the anti-aircraft guns.

With all the main armament grouped forward, the *Nelson* and *Rodney* were at first criticized for lack of astern fire. The merits of the arrangement, however, were not lost on the French Navy, which later built the basically similar, but somewhat smaller, *Dunkerque* and *Strasbourg.* These vessels grouped the main armament forward in two large quadruple turrets; their dual-purpose secondary armament replaced the separate anti-torpedo and anti-aircraft batteries of the British ships. The speed of the French ships was stepped up to 29½ knots, heralding the introduction of the fast battleship.

The two German vessels, the *Gneisenau* and *Scharnhorst,* were more conservative, with their main armament forward and aft. Although rated as battlecruisers, they sacrificed no armored protection to make 32 knots; neither did they sacrifice firepower. They carried 11-inch guns as there was no larger caliber available at the time (the intention was to rearm them later with twin 15-inch guns in place of the triple

A small U.S. battleship the
South Dakota (1942).

11-inch turrets). Both secondary and tertiary armaments were installed and the latter—14 heavy guns controlled by four high-angle optical directors—showed an appreciation of the air threat well in advance of other navies.

The fast battleship

When the Washington Treaty lapsed at the end of 1935 immediate construction began on new capital ships within the specified limits by all signatories except Japan, who refused to be bound by the 35,000-ton, 16-inch gun limit and thereafter drew a veil of secrecy over her activities.

All the new battleships aimed for high speed, incorporated adequate vertical and horizontal protective armor, improved

One of the largest American battleships, the *New Jersey* (1943), in action.

aerial defense, and aircraft for spotting and reconnaissance duties.

The United States Navy unhesitatingly went to the upper limit in firepower for the battleships *North Carolina* and *Washington,* arranging their nine 16-inch guns in triple turrets—two forward and one aft. The same arrangement was adopted by the Italians for the *Littorio* and *Vittorio Veneto,* but they used 15-inch guns as they wanted more speed. Fifteen-inch guns were also fitted to the French *Richelieu* and *Jean Bart* and the German *Bismarck* and *Tirpitz;* the former mounted their eight guns in two quadruple turrets forward, the latter grouped their guns in twin turrets forward and aft. The British Navy, already committed to the 14-inch gun, housed ten in two quadruple turrets in the *King George V* and *Prince of Wales,* arranging one turret forward and one aft, with a superimposed twin turret forward.

The succeeding American *South Dakota*-class battleships were similar to the *North Carolina* but were 50 feet shorter, while the *Iowa* class advanced to 45,000 tons and attained 33 knots, a speed unmatched by any other battleship or battle cruiser for that matter. The *U.S.S. Missouri,* launched in 1944, had a displacement of 53,000 tons.

Two more *Littorio*-class ships were built by the Italian Navy, but Germany never advanced its project for six 56,200-ton battleships with diesel engines and 16-inch guns.

Two more French vessels of the *Richelieu* class were never completed, and the final unit was modified with the quadruple turrets distributed forward and aft. Three more *King George V* class were built by the British Navy, but the following *Lion* class (which were all cancelled) reverted to 16-inch guns arranged as in the *North Carolina,* with a corresponding

The largest battleship ever built was the Japanese *Yamato* (1941), finally sunk by American naval aircraft.

rise in displacement to 40,000 tons. One other battleship, the *Vanguard,* was completed to utilize spare 15-inch turrets.

The Japanese giants

As noted earlier, strict secrecy shrouded Japanese naval construction after 1936 so that it was not until the end of World War II that accurate details became available.

Well aware that they would be unable to match American numerical supremacy in capital ships, the Japanese designed the *Yamato*-class ships to be individually superior to any battleship afloat. As a result, the vessels dwarfed contemporary ships of American and European construction. In all, five ships were projected, of which only the first two — the *Yamato* and *Musashi* — were completed as battleships. These ships were the ultimate in battleship design.

With a final standard displacement of 64,170 tons, they were designed to mount nine 18-inch guns in triple turrets, two forward and one aft; eight 8-inch guns in twin turrets disposed in lozenge fashion; and an anti-aircraft battery of twelve 5-inch guns in twin turrets and twenty-four 25-millimeter (one-inch) guns in triple shields. Six aircraft were carried aft with two training catapults at the stern. This armament was later modified.

Protection was on a massive scale with special attention to underwater damage; above the waterline the belt armor was applied externally but below it was behind the hull. The side was invulnerable to 18-inch gunfire at 20,000 yards and the deck to a 2,000-pound bomb dropped from 10,000 feet.

Main propulsion was provided by geared turbines of 150,000 shp, taking steam at 350 lb/in^2 and 800° F from twelve boilers, and driving four shafts for a speed of 27½ knots.

SEAPLANE AND AIRCRAFT CARRIERS

The seaplane carrier

Soon after the inception of the airplane, its value for reconnaissance was recognized. Fitted with floats, the plane was adapted for naval purposes.

To accommodate seaplanes, the earliest mother ship — the British seaplane carrier *Ark Royal* — was converted from a standard commercial coal-carrier with machinery arranged aft. The hull was modified and the holds were used for stowing the seaplanes, which were hoisted in and out by cranes. The seaplanes took off and landed on the water, but, as this was very much a smooth-water operation, their use was restricted by sea conditions.

By the outbreak of World War I aircraft had already assumed an offensive role and could carry either bombs or torpedoes. In 1914 the British Navy acquired and fitted out a number of fast cross-channel steamers as seaplane carriers. They were provided with a hangar and cranes aft, could carry four seaplanes, and were armed with four 12-pounder guns. One of these boats, the *Engadine,* was present at the battle of Jutland.

The limitations of water take-off and landing had been

realized before the war, and both the American and British navies had experimented with aircraft taking off from improvised runways fitted to anchored warships. In 1910 a wheeled aircraft took off from a flight deck fitted over the fore end of the American Cruiser *Birmingham,* and in the

British conversions during World War I: the seaplane carrier *Engadine* (*above*) and the aircraft carrier *Campania* (*below*).

following year another landed on an after flight deck on the battleship *Pennsylvania*. In the same year British aircraft became airborne from the runway on the fo'c'sle of the battleship *Africa*.

The early aircraft carrier

In 1914 the British Navy took over the liner *Campania* and fitted her with an inclined flight deck which ran from bridge to stem. When it was later found necessary to lengthen this deck, the fore funnel was split and the deck passed through it. The *Campania* was the first vessel to use a lift to transfer aircraft from the hangar deck to the flight deck. As the result of several years' experimental work, an aircraft was launched from a catapult fitted on the quarter-deck of the American armored cruiser *North Carolina* in 1915, while she was under way. The original intention behind the catapult

The British ship *Furious* is portrayed (*below*) after her second conversion to the role of aircraft carrier. The smaller picture is of later date and shows her after a third conversion.

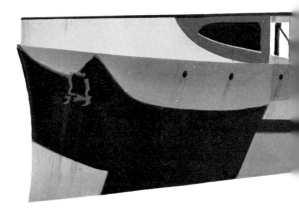

34

was to launch aircraft from warships not fitted with flight decks, but the catapult system was later to play an important part in the evolution of the aircraft carrier.

In 1917 the British cruiser *Furious* was modified when her forward 18-inch turret was removed and replaced with a small flight deck with hangar space below it. From this deck the first take-off and landing while under way were accomplished, the latter being particularly hazardous. A landing deck was provided the following year when the aft 18-inch turret was removed. The cruiser *Cavendish,* which was similarly converted and renamed *Vindictive,* showed the feasibility of this application to a smaller ship.

The separate take-off and landing decks of the *Furious* were a makeshift arrangement dictated by war expediency, and there were obvious disadvantages, such as the transfer outboard (off the side of the ship) of aircraft from the after to the

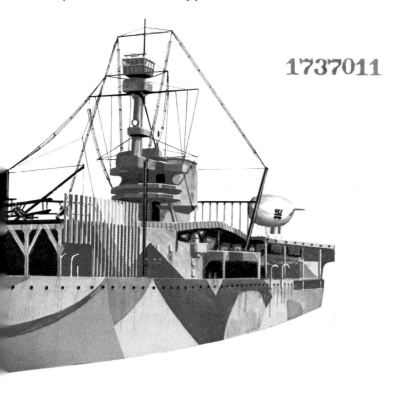

1737011

forward deck. But even before alterations had been effected the next bold step of providing a completely decked-over vessel had been planned. In selecting suitable ships for conversion the British Navy did not have a wide choice, and the incomplete hulls of the Chilean battleship *Almirante Cochrane* (renamed *Eagle*) and the Italian liner *Conte Rosso* (renamed *Argus*) were acquired by Britain for this purpose in 1916–17. Also, an order was placed for the first vessel specifically designed as a carrier, the *Hermes,* an example that was soon followed in Japan with the *Hosho.*

The *Argus* was completed first and was a flush-decked vessel with the smoke discharged at the stern through horizontal ducts along the side. For navigational purposes there was a retractable charthouse at the fore end of the flight deck with small bridge positions on each side. A novel arrangement, however, was adopted by the *Eagle;* the bridge

Sopwith Pup aircraft circling above the British carrier *Argus,* converted from an Italian liner during World War I.

and funnels were fitted as an island superstructure on the starboard (right side, facing the bow) side of the flight deck. Experience showed that this was a preferable arrangement and it is the one that still persists in modern carriers. Both vessels had hangars below the flight deck which were connected by center-line lifts.

There was considerable interest in the *Hermes* (10,850 tons) and the *Hosho* (9,494 tons), the first custom-built carriers. They were both much smaller than the *Argus* (14,450 tons) and the *Eagle* (22,600 tons), and yet they were able to stow just as many aircraft. The only American example at this particular time was the flush-decked carrier *Langley* (ex-*Jupiter*) which had been converted from a fleet coal-carrier. She carried her aircraft partly dismantled in the holds, from which they were hoisted by cranes to the upper deck and then transferred by lift to the flight deck. The *Langley* could, however, stow 55 aircraft, a considerable increase over the 20 carried by the British vessels; she was fitted with a catapult because her slow speed was inadequate to provide the necessary wind speed for take-off.

Conversions from capital ships

As a result of the Washington Naval Treaty there were numerous cancellations in capital ship construction, and many of these hulls were converted to aircraft carriers. Both Japan and the United States retained two battle cruiser hulls for this purpose, and France the hull of a battleship. The terms of the treaty, however, determined that the British cruisers *Courageous* and *Glorious* would have to be included in the total tonnage allocated to capital ships if retained as armed. This was highly undesirable, so they were put in hand for conversion to carriers, together with the *Furious*, which was to undergo a third major alteration. Following the earthquake

disaster of 1923 the Japanese plans were modified as one of the battle cruiser hulls was so damaged that it had to be scrapped and replaced by the hull of a cancelled battleship.

The first of these conversions to pass into service was the British *Furious* in 1925. Although the forward take-off deck was still retained, a large flight deck was added at a higher level abaft (sternward from) it and extended unobstructed to the stern. Smoke was discharged aft (sternward) through horizontal ducts and navigational arrangements similar to those in the *Argus* (see page 36)—a retractable charthouse and wing bridge positions—were adopted. The use of the forward take-off deck was eventually discontinued.

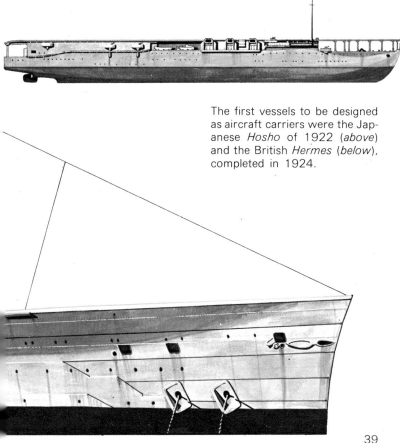

The first vessels to be designed as aircraft carriers were the Japanese *Hosho* of 1922 (*above*) and the British *Hermes* (*below*), completed in 1924.

Two years later the American carriers, the *Lexington* and the *Saratoga*, were completed. For many years they were the largest carriers in the world. They adopted the *Eagle's* island arrangement (see pp. 36 and 37), with a large starboard funnel, mounting eight 8-inch guns in twin turrets forward and aft of the starboard island superstructure. The original battlecruiser turbo-electric machinery was retained and their sustained 33 knots set a standard only recently surpassed.

The French *Béarn* was not outstanding, since the French Navy lacked previous experience in this field. With a speed of only 21½ knots and a radius of action on the low side the *Béarn* was restricted to operating mainly with the battlefleet.

The first Japanese vessel, the *Akagi*, was flush decked and similar to the British *Furious* except that two take-off decks —one above and behind the other—were provided forward, followed by the main flight deck at a higher level. The funnel arrangement was grotesque: the main exhaust projected horizontally from the starboard side and was turned down at its outboard end, while the auxiliary exhaust was trunked out at the ship's side and positioned vertically with its top at flight-deck level. She was armed with 8-inch guns; there were twin turrets to port and starboard on the lower forward

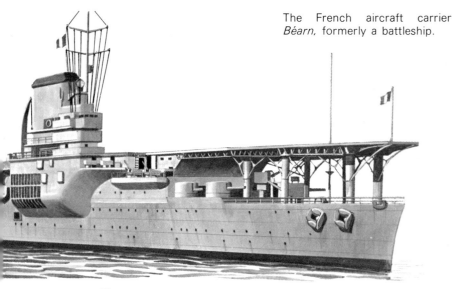

The French aircraft carrier *Béarn,* formerly a battleship.

The American aircraft carrier *Lexington*, an ex-battle cruiser, could steam at 33 knots.

take-off deck and three guns on each side aft in main-deck armored casemates. The *Kaga*, which followed, was similar except that smoke was led aft through horizontal ducts running along the side, and she was a little slower as her installed power (intended for a battleship) was lower.

Finally, the British pair, the *Courageous* and the *Glorious*, were very similar to the *Furious* and benefited by experience gained with her. The take-off deck forward was retained, but it was never used for this purpose; the island arrangement was adopted for bridge and funnels, and the gun armament was restricted to defensive anti-aircraft guns.

The fleet aircraft carrier

It must be emphasized that the effectiveness of a carrier was firmly linked to the efficiency of its air group. Superior ship performance on its own was not enough; it had to be matched — if not exceeded — by the performance of its aircraft, otherwise it was like arming a new battleship with muzzle-loading guns. Here, the Japanese and United States navies were fortunate in retaining control of their own air services, unlike other navies, such as that of Britain. A basic difference in carrier philosophies developed. The British Navy looked to its carriers only to provide air superiority over its own fleet while acting in concert with it; but the United States Navy evolved the task force concept, with its carriers securing air superiority over the enemy fleet while detached from, although acting with, its own fleet. The task-force concept was more flexible because it could be adapted to other offensive tactics. The defensive British attitude, however, visualized carriers being detached only for the purpose of merchant convoy duties. The United States Navy, with aircraft development firmly in its control, could plan ahead, while the British Royal Navy was stymied with the reins in hands other than its own. The Japanese carrier philosophy also evolved along American lines.

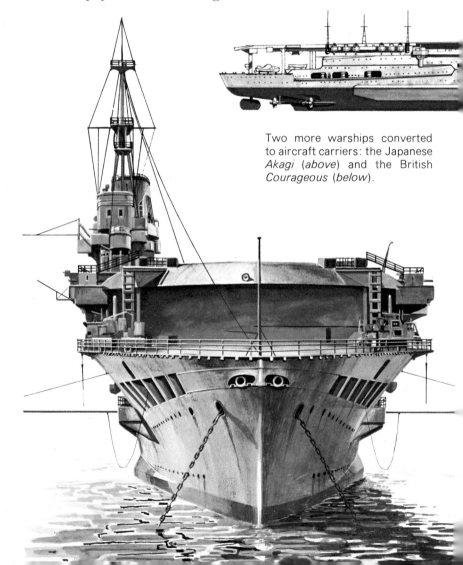

Two more warships converted to aircraft carriers: the Japanese *Akagi* (*above*) and the British *Courageous* (*below*).

Not unnaturally, the experience gained from this varied collection of carriers influenced future designs. Under the terms of the Washington Naval Treaty aircraft carriers were limited in size and total tonnage; they were defined as vessels between 10,000 and 27,000 tons so that below the lesser displacement they did not rank as carriers and were excluded from the total tonnage figure. The Japanese Navy took full advantage of this clause in designing the *Ryujo*, which was laid down in 1929 as an 8,000-ton vessel with a

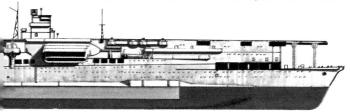

single hangar. However, during her construction, the first London Naval Treaty (1930) closed this loophole, and the *Ryujo's* design was modified to improve her combatant value. A second hangar deck was added to increase aircraft capacity; when this affected her stability, the Japanese reduced her defensive armament. The *Ryujo* was therefore never a wholly satisfactory vessel, but she had a novel arrangement for the bridge, which was sited well forward below the fore end of the flight deck.

In 1931 the United States Navy laid down the medium-sized *Ranger*, in which the main design feature was aircraft capacity, showing a true appreciation of her function. Consequently, the *Ranger* was slower and less well-protected than her contemporaries. Although she had an island superstructure, the boiler uptakes were led to six hinged funnels well aft which were lowered to a horizontal position during flying operations. The *Yorktown*, laid down four years later, was slightly larger and incorporated all-around improvements. Her speed and radius were increased, protection improved, and the machinery placed amidships so that the funnel formed part of the island superstructure.

The *Soryu*, a vessel basically similar to the *Yorktown*, was laid down by the Japanese Navy in the same year and illus-

The U.S. carrier
Coral Sea (1947)

trated the parallel development taking place in both navies. A sister ship, the *Hiryu*, experimented with the island placed on the port side, but its funnel uptakes were still brought up to starboard. This configuration only increased the air disturbance over the flight deck.

In 1935 the British started work on the *Ark Royal*. She proved a worthy contemporary of the American and Japanese vessels but was larger, had a heavier defensive armament and was better protected with armor. The hull plating was extended to the flight deck, which made her very dry forward, and she was unmatched for seaworthiness.

The *Wasp,* a diminutive of the *Yorktown* class, was laid down in 1936 by the United States Navy and was especially interesting. She had athwartship catapults fitted at hangar-deck level, in addition to the more usual fore-and-aft catapults at the fore end of the flight deck, and a deck-edge elevator. The former encroached on, and the latter saved, hangar-deck space, so the first was abandoned and the second retained.

The next year four units of the *Illustrious* class were laid down by the British Navy, and their outstanding feature was that the whole hangar structure—deck, sides and roof— became an armored box incorporated with the hull. The

A British Fairey Gannet aircraft stowed on the lift of a carrier.

penalty was that only a single hangar could be provided and the aircraft capacity (compared with *Ark Royal*) was halved. However, it ensured survival in areas where carriers were exposed to heavy air attack. Later, the aircraft capacity was increased by accepting deck-stowed planes and by incorporating a half-hangar in the last unit. Two further vessels were very similar and incorporated the half-hangar from the outset, but the side armor was much reduced in thickness.

Two Japanese carriers laid down in the same year were expansions of the *Soryu* design. Now that all treaty limitations had lapsed, the United States Navy with the *Essex* class—started in 1941—advanced to dimensions approaching those of the battle cruiser conversions. Although aircraft capacity remained on a par with earlier carriers they were all able to operate larger and heavier aircraft, but with more tonnage devoted to ship performance.

Japan, however, undertook secret carrier construction that went undetected. Several years earlier the Japanese Imperial Navy planned a series of fast auxiliary vessels suitable for conversion to carriers. We now know that two submarine depot ships and one mercantile liner conversion were placed in service during 1941 and were joined, in the following year, by conversions from another depot ship and four more liners. Therefore, over a very short period, the Japanese Navy was able to double its carrier strength. While these conversions did not match the more recent fleet vessels, the availability of 16 carriers proved crucial to Japan's success early in World War II.

Before the outbreak of World War II, France and Germany also embarked on carrier construction. The French vessels had the flight decks offset to port, and, while comparable in size to the *Yorktown* and the *Soryu,* they had only half their aircraft capacity. German carrier construction was hampered at every turn by inexperience and the German Luftwaffe's complete lack of cooperation with the navy. Designed to operate in concert with raiding capital ship squadrons, much of the German carrier's tonnage was devoted to ship features, with a corresponding reduction in aircraft capacity. The German plans omitted a heavy armament of low-angle and high-angle guns. The carriers were to be fast, with an adequate radius of action. However, only one German carrier, the *Graf Zeppelin,* reached the launching stage.

The escort aircraft carrier

When exposed to the test of war, the carrier soon asserted itself with telling effect, as shown by the British at Taranto, the Japanese at Pearl Harbor and the United States at Midway. In the Pacific, as early as 1942, the carrier had become the capital unit around which a task force was formed. But even earlier the carrier had proved itself in the Atlantic convoy battle.

Outside the range of shore-based Allied maritime aircraft on both sides of the Atlantic was a wide reach of sea in which convoys were deprived of air cover unless a carrier was available. Fleet carriers were far too few and valuable to be exposed to this

American escort carriers: a *Prince William*-class unit (*above*) and the *Long Island* of 1941 (*below*).

duty. A smaller, slower, unsophisticated vessel proved adequate — the escort carrier, which needed only to house a small number of reconnaissance-bomber and fighter planes.

The prototype of the escort carrier, the British ship *Audacity,* was converted from a captured German merchant vessel in 1940. Her superstructure was cut down and a flight deck added; she stowed six planes on her deck and made 15 knots. Under the terms of the 'Lend/Lease' agreement negotiated between America and Britain prior to America's entry into the war, the United States quickly provided ten similar conversions for convoy duty on the North Atlantic. After America entered the conflict, production of the escort carrier was stepped up. By the war's end, 113 of the ships had been put into service. For the *Casablanca*-class escort carrier, which saw much service, the building time was cut from eight months to three-and-a-half months. It took only 366 days for the whole class of 55 units to be commissioned.

In comparison the Japanese output was small and only four further conversions were effected—two from mercantile liners and two from naval seaplane carriers. However, as they were for front-line duty their conversions were much more elaborate. Both the Italian and German navies proposed mercantile conversions during the war but none ever came to fruition, although the Italian *Aquila* reached an advanced stage of construction.

The merchant aircraft carrier
Until the American escort-carrier program was in full swing a British project was introduced as an interim measure: the merchant aircraft carrier (MAC). The conversion could be undertaken only with cargo ships that could dispense with

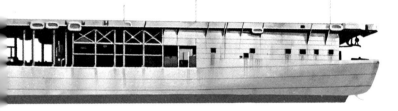

the normal cargo hatches; six grain carriers and four tankers were altered during construction and nine other tankers (two under the Dutch flag) were converted. The original Admiralty specification had called for a speed of 14 or 15 knots and a flight deck measuring 490 × 62 feet, but this was reduced to 11 knots and 390 × 62 feet so that standard war cargo hulls could be used. The grain carriers were provided with a hangar and an elevator, which could be omitted from the longer tankers whose after flight decks served as a permanent deck park for aircraft. Both types carried four aircraft and a naval air complement but were otherwise manned by merchant seamen. They were used both as merchant ships and aircraft carriers during an early period of the war.

A somewhat similar plan was adopted in Japan toward the close of the war with five tankers then under construction. But because of a shortage of fuel oil, Japan had to revert to coal-firing vessels that took on their supplies of coal through main-deck hatches. Such ships proved impossible to deck for the operation of aircraft while also performing as merchant haulers.

War construction
In the United States, the construction of fleet aircraft carriers — the new capital ship — greatly intensified after the outbreak of World War II. Britain, America's major naval ally, could not undertake any large-scale program because of her more limited resources and, by then, her total dependence upon the United States for carrier aircraft. Still, the British projected four enlarged *Illustrious*-class carriers (pp. 45–46), with double hangars and full armor, as well as three giant 45,000-ton carriers. Although two of the former were laid down, all the larger units were eventually cancelled.

The United States had become largely dependent on fleet carriers for the war in the Pacific. The *Essex* class (p. 46) was expanded to 32 ships. The subsequent *Midway* class, much bigger at 45,000 tons, was armored on the British principle (p. 45). At the war's end, in 1945, eight *Essex*-class and three *Midway*-class units were abruptly cancelled.

Carriers were equally critical to the Japanese, but shortages in most essential construction materials crippled Japan's

production. Although ambitious programs were proposed, they remained paper projects with no hope of fulfillment.

The *Taiho,* laid down shortly before the Japanese bombed Pearl Harbor, emerged as the only unit of her type, although more were planned. The main features of the *Taiho*—a single armored hangar and a strong defensive armament—bore a close resemblance to those of the British *Illustrious.* Unlike the usual horizontal arrangement, the funnel was stepped vertically but it was nevertheless inclined outboard at a bizarre angle.

Another Japanese wartime completion was the *Shinano,* which had been laid down as a battleship of the *Yamato* class and was converted to a carrier while being built. Despite her bulk—she greatly surpassed even the 45,000-ton American *Midway* class—the *Shinano's* striking power was limited by Japan's acute shortage of planes and pilots. She was provided with ample facilities for refueling aircraft from other carriers, but Japan's intent to use her as a support platform was frustrated by her premature loss.

Japan's *Unryu* class, which reverted to the smaller dimensions and general arrangement of the *Hiryu* (page 44), was more realistic. But, of 17 vessels planned, the last 11 were not even laid down. In fact, the *Unryu* class em-

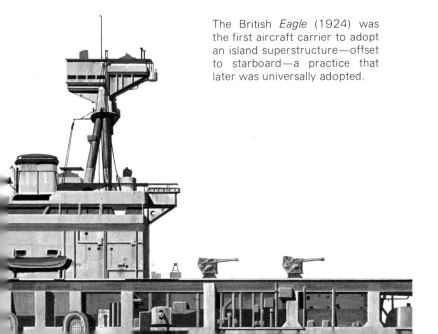

The British *Eagle* (1924) was the first aircraft carrier to adopt an island superstructure—offset to starboard—a practice that later was universally adopted.

bodied the Japanese solution to a problem that also beset the United States Navy: to shorten the time for construction and trials of a fleet carrier. In the critical years of 1942–43, the United States Navy, unable to wait on long-term construction, had instituted a crash program for the construction of light fleet carriers.

The light fleet carrier

In the United States, the most suitable hulls available for rapid conversion to light fleet carriers were those of the *Cleveland*-class light cruisers; nine—all constructed in one yard—were selected for this purpose. The original machinery in the hold remained unaltered, but deep bulges were added to the hull to improve stability. Four short, paired funnels distinguished their silhouettes. Although they were restricted both in capacity and in the type of aircraft that could be stowed, they nevertheless proved effective stopgaps.

Similar conversions were undertaken with the cruisers *Seydlitz* and *Ibuki* by Germany and Japan. These, however, were still uncompleted at the end of the war.

The light fleet carrier was also adopted by Britain, with the essential difference that it had to be built from scratch. In 1939 the aircraft maintenance carrier *Unicorn,* which was designed to service shipborne aircraft, had been laid down. While she was decked for landing and take-off purposes, she carried no aircraft of her own. Below decks she housed workshops and stores for her support task. Although the *Unicorn* would have proved most useful in this support role, she was nevertheless completed as an operational carrier and served as a model for Britain's subsequent light fleet carriers. To reduce building time, their hulls were constructed to previously proven design requirements, and simple, rugged and austere standards were adopted throughout. Two very

A Hurricane aircraft being catapulted from a specially fitted British merchant ship during World War II.

similar classes, totaling 16 vessels, were ordered. Two were completed as maintenance carriers and one other was never finished. Although these British wartime vessels had their shortcomings, seven are still in service today with the navies of Argentina, Australia, Brazil, Canada, France, India and the Netherlands.

The aircraft carrier in the atomic age

With the advent of the atomic bomb the survival of the aircraft carrier—like all major surface warships—was put in jeopardy because so obvious a target as a carrier task force would invite nuclear attack. The problems associated with fleet air defense were not insuperable, however. Measures that could easily be implemented were greater fleet dispersal and earlier detection and improved interception of the attacker. By the late 1940's, therefore, the resilient carrier, though vulnerable, was difficult to detect and hard to destroy. Nor should it be forgotten that carrier aircraft could also deliver atomic bombs, and the ability to strike back in kind was in itself a deterrent to attack.

Both the United States and Britain have contributed to improved flight-deck operations. The angled deck, the mirror landing aid, and the steam catapult, originally British innovations, make it possible to launch and recover aircraft simultaneously, accommodate higher landing speeds safely and launch the much heavier aircraft now in operation. To these advances the United States added deck-edge airplane elevators and deck parks so that the flight deck, formerly a fairly regular rectangle, today assumes an irregular shape. With the island superstructure still to starboard, the angled deck is run off to port. Four deck-edge airplane elevators are fitted amidships, three to starboard and one to port, and four catapults are provided, two each at the forward ends of the angled deck and flight deck.

The type of aircraft operated determines the size of the flight deck. With the 800 feet required by modern jet aircraft, the carrier has continued to increase in size. Not sur-

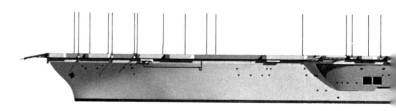

Profile and aerial view of the American nuclear-powered aircraft carrier *Enterprise* (1961). She carries up to 100 aircraft.

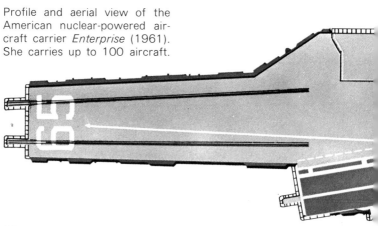

prisingly, displacement has risen from 59,600 tons with the American *Forrestal*—the first postwar-designed carrier—to the 75,700 tons of the nuclear-powered *Enterprise,* currently the largest class of carrier afloat. The latter's eight nuclear reactors generate the steam for four sets of geared steam turbines totaling 360,000 horsepower. Achieving speeds around 36 knots, the *Enterprise* has an unlimited high-speed endurance. For defensive purposes the *Enterprise* primarily relies on her own aircraft, together with the weapons of her accompanying escorts. Her armament also includes guided-missile anti-aircraft systems. Her high speed is her best defense against submarines. She can be completely replenished at sea by a fleet of fast support ships. Until manned aircraft are completely supplanted by missiles, there appears little likelihood of the carrier becoming obsolete, and she has amply demonstrated her ability over the past 20 years.

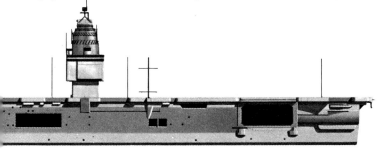

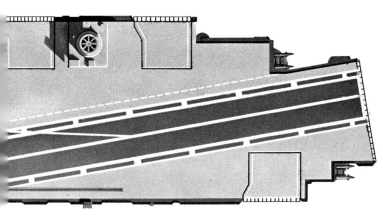

Despatch vessels: the British *Iris*
(*above*) of 1879 and the Japanese *Mogami* (*below*) of 1907.

CRUISERS

The iron frigate and corvette

Historically, the main functions of the cruiser were to scout
for the battlefleet, to protect trade and—before wireless te-
legraphy—to repeat signals and carry urgent despatches. For
all these duties the cruiser required speed together with a
long radius of action. Therefore, the 19th-century adoption
of steam propulsion was of more importance to the cruiser
than was the use of armor plate. The use of metal eventually
meant that the hull could be longer and lighter. Neither advance was forgotten in the desire to secure high speed.

Cruiser requirements varied considerably among different navies. The development of the cruiser is best studied
among the maritime nations which had overseas possessions
and were therefore dependent on maintaining communications and protecting trade; the navies of such countries
required cruisers of all types.

The earliest iron frigates were large and fast (the British *Inconstant,* at 5,780 tons, steamed at 16 knots) and they were, of course, fully rigged. As they were too costly to build in large numbers, most navies adopted a smaller iron corvette of slightly less speed. In both cases the armament was still carried on the broadside with manually operated light chase guns at the bow and stern.

Smaller than the corvette, and with a good turn of speed, was the despatch vessel. It was very lightly armed as its machinery absorbed a large proportion of the available weight and space. As early as 1879 the British *Iris* was steaming at 18 knots and, at the time, was the world's fastest warship.

The submerged armored deck

At first, cruisers remained dependent upon sail for long sea voyages and used their steam only in calms or on entering action. Since the cruiser's speed was its chief virtue, designers were loathe to weight her down with armor. However,

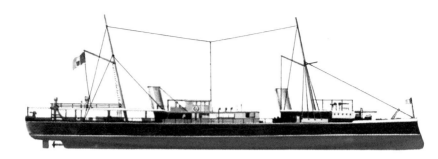

wooden cruisers operating at remote stations were more frequently being challenged by small ironclads steaming in close proximity to home waters. This was particularly true for a nation like Britain, whose fleets often patroled the coasts of rival powers. The wooden cruiser was no match for even small ironclad coast-defense vessels, and so Britain laid down the new ironclad *Shannon*, with armored gun positions fore and aft, and—a totally new feature—a submerged armored deck fitted horizontally beneath the main wood deck to shield the machinery in the hold against short-range, flat-trajectory plunging fire (see page 22).

Once the full rig was abandoned and breech-loading guns were introduced, there was marked progress in the cruiser's development. A fully rigged corvette with a partially armored deck over the machinery spaces that could make 13 knots was, within a few years, matched by a twin-screw vessel with a complete armored deck able to steam at 16 knots. Although the sides of the armored deck still remained below the waterline, the crown was arched to slightly above the waterline so that there was more headroom in the boiler and engine rooms. This countered the objection that with the side pierced suffi-

Torpedo cruisers: the Italian *Partenope* of 1890 (*above*) and the British *Scout* (*below*), completed in 1885.

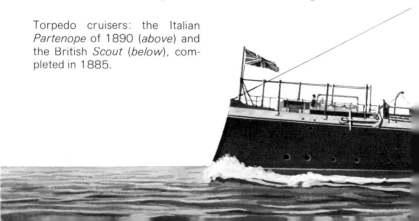

cient water could collect over the flat armored deck to affect stability because, with the crown arched, water would be restricted to narrow channels along each side.

The general arrangement of cruising vessels largely followed traditional practice, with a fo'c'sle and poop decks joined by a high bulwark behind which guns were carried on the broadside. Cruisers retained the broadside system longer than battleships as it better suited their type of action. They would generally make the first contact with the enemy on the fringes of their respective fleets and, in the ensuing *mêlée*, it was more than likely that they would be engaged with enemy vessels on both sides.

The Elswick cruiser

In 1885 British industry completed the cruiser *Esmeralda* for Chile. Fo'c'sle, poop and bulwark went by the board; heavy 10-inch, 25-ton chase guns were positioned fore and aft and the medium 6-inch, 4-ton guns amidships; protection was afforded by a complete armored deck; and a speed of over 18 knots was realized. All this was achieved on a displacement of under 3,000 tons, and for the next 20 years the Elswick cruiser was to be a pace-setter synonymous with heavy armament

and high speed on a small displacement.

The torpedo cruiser
The torpedo cruiser was conceived as an ocean-going torpedo boat—a sound idea, somewhat ahead of its time. The speed and frailty of the torpedo boat were sacrificed for a larger and more seaworthy hull, and the vessel carried about ten fixed torpedo tubes in the bow and stern and on the broadside, with only a light gun armament on the fo'c'sle and poop. As it was rather heavily loaded for its 1,500-ton displacement the torpedo cruiser soon lost speed in a rough sea and could seldom close to effective torpedo range on the high seas except in fine weather.

There is little use for a cruiser that cannot operate in both good and bad weather, thus the type appeared only briefly on the cruiser scene. A main armament of torpedoes was never adapted for general capital-ship service.

The armored cruiser

Before the turn of the century, any nation's construction of a cruiser that could be used against trade usually resulted in an immediate counter by the British Navy, owing to the absolute dependence of the British Empire on sea communications.

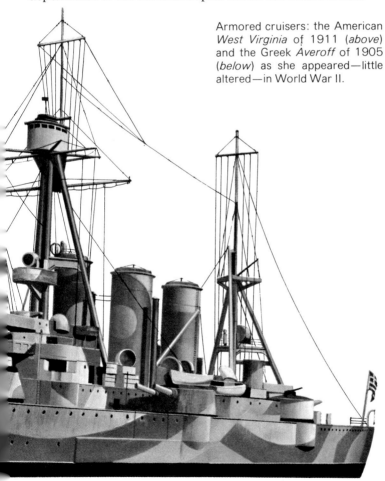

Armored cruisers: the American *West Virginia* of 1911 (*above*) and the Greek *Averoff* of 1905 (*below*) as she appeared—little altered—in World War II.

The typical commerce-raiding cruiser—or corsair—was a large ship with an armament including heavy guns. It possessed speed and a long radius of action, thanks to a combination of steam and sail propulsion. With her colonial lifelines menaced by foreign corsair construction, Great Britain resorted to a new class of large cruisers, which she built with an eye to safeguarding her trans-oceanic trade routes. The *Orlando*-class armored cruiser was almost as formidable as a battleship. Along the hull amidships ran a partial belt of armor 10 inches thick. This belt was boxed at the ends by means of 16-inch-thick iron bulkheads that cut athwartships (connecting the belt on one side of the hull to that on the other side). In the hold within this armored enclosure were fitted triple steam-expansion engines (piston-type engines) that gave the cruiser an added 1,000 horsepower and a top speed of 19 knots. In order to squeeze the machinery beneath the waterline (for added protection), the engines were fitted horizontally. Above the machinery, submerged deck armor served as a shield against plunging fire, which was not yet the problem it would be once long-range action became possible with improved range-finding methods. The cruiser had an armored conning tower, or bridge, and armored gun shields. She carried 9.2-inchers fore and aft, and ten 6-inchers amidships.

The classification of cruisers

In 1908, Britain convened the London Naval Conference, which was attended by the world's leading maritime powers. The idea was to try to arrive at a treaty for the limitation of armaments. A classification system for rating warships, according to their tonnage and armament, was proposed, and quotas were suggested to limit the construction of warships of various classes. The highest classification was that of capital ship. The battleship fell into this class, but so did some heavy armored cruisers. Armored cruisers below capital-ship size were subject to another quota. Still lighter cruisers—frigates, corvettes, sloops, despatch vessels and torpedo cruisers—were assigned ratings as first-, second- and third-class protected (armored) ships, each class governed by set quotas.

Much controversy surrounded the mode of armoring. Seamen preferred external plate that gave broad protection, since internal deck armor let shell penetrate the hull

Two 2nd-class protected cruisers: the Italian *Etna* of 1887 (*above*) and the British vessel *Leander* (*below*), completed in 1885.

before offering resistance. Naval planners, however, leaned toward the armored deck. It protected the machinery without greatly increasing the tonnage, with the effect of raising a cruiser's classification. Thus treaty politics complicated the cruiser's development.

The protected cruiser

Two years after the *Orlando* was laid down, the British Navy started work on the *Blake*, which had a maximum speed of 22 knots and a large radius so that she could surpass all regular, or auxiliary, cruisers used against trade. The armament was the same as the *Orlando's* but there was a great increase in size to accommodate more powerful machinery and an enlarged coal bunker. The *Blake* had the first vertical triple expansion engines to be installed in a cruiser. As the cylinder tops of the engines would have projected above the armored deck, the deck was arched and sloped to enclose them. At this time the first quick-firing guns were coming into service. Given the rapidity of their salvos, they were more likely to score a

hit at long range—raising the danger of plunging fire (see page 22). This may have influenced the departure from side armor; for the total weight of armor for the much larger *Blake* was 1,190 tons, the smaller *Orlando's,* 960 tons.

Most 2nd- and 3rd-class protected cruisers retained the arrangement of a short fo'c'sle and poop, on which the chase guns were mounted, with the remaining guns in the waist on each side. Usually the 2nd-class vessel had 6-inch chase guns and 6-inch or 4.7-inch guns in the waist, whereas the 3rd-class vessel had a uniform battery of 4.7-inch or 4-inch guns. Maximum speeds were about 20 knots in 2nd-class vessels and 18 knots in 3rd-class vessels.

Cruiser design remained much the same, with no marked increase in speed, until the advent of the British battleship *Dreadnought* forced the issue. There were, however, lively disputes over the introduction of forced draft and watertube boilers.

The destruction and protection of commerce

Among the world's noteworthy turn-of-the-century cruisers were the French *Dupuy de Lome* (1890), the American *Columbia* (1892), and the Russian *Rurik* (1894), all of which were corsairs. The *Dupuy de Lôme,* at 6,300 tons, carried all her main and secondary guns in turrets and was protected by 4-inch armor along the entire hull to the upper deck. The main

The British 3rd-class protected cruiser *Pelorus* (1897)

190-millimeter (7.5-inch) guns were placed on each side amidships and sponsored out for full 180-degree arcs on their respective sides; the secondary 160-millimeter (6.2-inch) guns were arranged three at each end with wide arcs across the bow and stern. With a speed of 20 knots, some two or three knots below foreign contemporaries, the *Dupuy de Lôme* was more prepared to fight it out than to avoid action.

The 7,475-ton *Columbia,* on the other hand, was prepared to use her high speed of 22 knots to avoid action rather than join it with her light armament of one 8-inch, two 6-inch, and eight 4-inch guns. However, both her speed and armament were adequate for overhauling and sinking even the fastest merchant vessels by gunfire. The slowest of the trio, the *Rurik,* could make 18 knots and, surprisingly, was fully rigged. With a displacement of 10,923 tons, she fairly bristled with guns and, if brought to action, could bring four 8-inch, sixteen 6-inch, and six 4.7-inch guns to bear. While the *Columbia* was deck-protected, the *Rurik* was protected by a narrow waterline belt, and in both of them all the gun positions were unarmored.

The *Rurik* prompted the construction of the British *Powerful* and *Terrible,* whose dimensions — 14,200 tons and 538 feet — surpassed even contemporary battleships. They easily made 22 knots but needed 48 new Belleville boilers to supply the

The French armored cruiser *Dupuy de Lôme* (1895).

steam. These boilers were of the modern watertube, or coil, type and started a bitter dispute about their merits. As a result, there was a series of competitive tests between cruisers with watertube and traditional cylindrical boilers; the most interesting outcome was the discovery that cruising distance was not limited by coal capacity but by the amount of reserve feed water carried to make up water losses in the boilers. In the end, the watertube boiler showed its superiority and was used in all high-powered warships.

Toward the close of the century there was an unexplained revival in armored cruiser construction. They were such large and costly vessels that consideration was even given to incorporating them in the line-of-battle, almost — it would appear — to justify their existence. But whatever the reason, they were built by most major navies and were acquired by a few minor navies. The Italian design found much favor abroad, and four were purchased by Argentina, one by Spain, and two by Japan. Such was the demand that the name *Giuseppe Garibaldi* was given to four vessels before it finally appeared in the Italian fleet, as the first three were all sold prior to completion! The armored cruiser was made obsolete by the battle cruiser which, armed with guns of battleship caliber, was finally drawn into the battleline.

The British 1st-class protected cruiser *Powerful* (1897) was larger than contemporary battleships.

The light cruiser

When the battleship *Dreadnought* increased the speed of the battlefleet by some three knots there had to be a similar rise in the speed of fleet cruisers. Fortunately the turbine, which enabled the *Dreadnought* to achieve this increase, was also available to the cruiser, and it led to such a rapid all-around development in design that there was a clear line of demarcation between the turbine cruiser and its earlier reciprocating- (or pistoned-) engined counterpart.

With armored and 1st-class protected cruisers obsolete, development stemmed from the 2nd- and 3rd-class cruisers. Thus, on about 5,000 tons displacement, the 2nd-class turbine cruiser made 25 knots, adhered to deck protection, carried about ten or twelve guns (either of uniform 4-inch caliber or with heavier 6-inch bow and stern chase pieces), and was suitable for work with the fleet or on the trade routes. The 3rd-class turbine cruisers were similar except that they averaged about 3,500 tons, had up to ten 4-inch guns, and were used either as scouts or as leaders for the destroyer flotillas.

The introduction of oil fuel started fresh developments at the 3rd-class rating, about 3,500 tons. But these ships carried armament comparable to the 2nd-class cruiser, with speed increased to 30 knots. However, the cruiser now lost the protection that had been afforded by its own coal, which had been arranged over and at the ends and sides of the machinery spaces. To compensate, thin side armor was used together with a partially armored deck. These vessels were first classed as light armored cruisers to distinguish them from the old type of armored cruiser, and later simply as light cruisers, to include the earlier turbine cruisers.

The combination of turbines and oil fuel marked a significant stage in cruiser design and resulted in fast and well-armed vessels of moderate size. They came through World War I with an enhanced reputation that was worthily earned in action. The height of their development is best exemplified by the British *Ceres* class which, at 4,200 tons, could steam at 29 knots, were sheathed in two to three inches of armor, and armed with five 6-inch guns all mounted on the center-line —two forward, one amidships and two aft—with the inboard end guns superimposed (see page 20).

The British *Amethyst,* (*bottom*) brought turbine propulsion to 3rd-class protected cruisers. (*Below*) The Austro-Hungarian *Novarra* (1914).

The *Ceres* 'C' class was slightly surpassed by the 'D' class, at 4,650 tons. Two subsequent classes were constructed to special wartime requirements:* the 'E' class, which weighed 7,550 tons and attained 33 knots, and the *Raleigh* class, enlarged to 9,750 tons to mount 7.5-inch guns.

The Washington cruiser

In framing the Washington Naval Treaty (1921–22), the convened powers placed an upper limit on cruisers at 10,000 tons and 8-inch guns. A ship exceeding these limits was classified as a capital ship, for which quotas were established. Any nation surpassing its quota supposedly must scrap some of its ships. This hurt Britain, for its latest series of cruisers exceeded the 10,000-ton limit, and they were considered as part of Britain's quota of capital ships and aircraft carriers. The United States and Japan insisted on keeping the 10,000-ton limit, and with France and Italy neutral, there was no sympathy for the British case to further revise the cruiser's restrictions.

*These requirements were based on war intelligence that the Germans were building fast cruisers and that they intended to fit heavy guns to their mercantile raiders. This information proved false but by that time the ships were so well advanced that only one unit (an 'E' class) could be cancelled.

With the first series of treaty cruisers the French and Italian navies secured high speed by sacrificing protection. Japan settled for less speed, arming its ships with an added twin 8-inch turret—making ten 8-inch guns. Japan's cruisers were more heavily armored, exceeding the treaty limit by about 1,000 tons. The British ships were slower than the French and Italian vessels but with no compensation in protection or armament. The Americans, last in the field, put ten guns into their ships, like Japan, but mounted them in two triple and two twin turrets. Their ships had good speed, armament and protection,

The Spanish heavy cruiser *Canarias* (1936).

yet were nearly 1,000 tons under the limit imposed by the treaty.

In the second series of treaty cruisers, enhanced protection, at the cost of speed, was incorporated by France and Italy (the latter also going over the limit); improvements were only marginal in Japan and Great Britain; and the United States

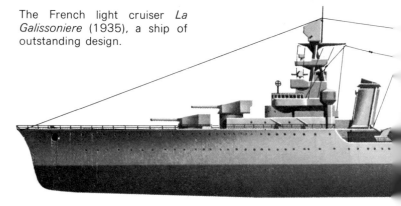

The French light cruiser *La Galissoniere* (1935), a ship of outstanding design.

created a new design around three triple 8-inch gun turrets.

Substantial protection without loss of speed was the feature of the third series. France and Italy produced singular examples, the United States equally good vessels, and Spain two vessels which were built to a British design. The first breakaway from the 10,000-ton type was made by Britain, which

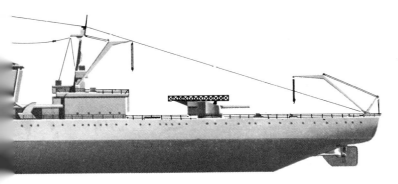

built two lighter cruisers by sacrificing a twin 8-inch turret aft. Two similar vessels were built for Argentina by Italy. All the treaty cruisers used side and deck armor except the first two series of British vessels, which were only deck protected. The French *Algérie* was the best example of the treaty type. Although some 25 percent of her weight was devoted to protection, she steamed at 31 knots, had a good radius of action and a strong anti-aircraft battery.

The London cruiser
The first London Naval Treaty (1930) brought a halt to the construction of 8-inch gun, 10,000-ton cruisers. The limitations on total tonnage were revised so that each navy could interpret its requirements as it chose. Construction now turned to smaller types of vessels armed with 6-inch guns, and they proved very effective. They were generally not extreme examples of any particular feature but a well-balanced compromise including some of the best examples of naval architecture.

The European navies all favored ships of about 7,000 tons, armed with eight or nine 6-inch guns, but Japan—who had always favored the large cruiser—forced the pace much as Britain had with the *Dreadnought* class 30 years earlier. Japan modified the heavy cruiser design by replacing twin 8-inch turrets with triple 6-inch turrets; thus, the *Mogami* class had 15 guns—nearly double the broadside of contemporary European ships. The British countered with the *Southampton* class (9,100 tons and twelve 6-inch guns), and the United States followed suit with the *Brooklyn* class (10,000 tons and fifteen 6-inch guns).

The German armored cruiser

In 1933 the German Navy completed the armored ship *Deutschland*. She complied with the Treaty of Versailles (1919) in that she was ostensibly a 10,000-ton (actually 11,700-ton) ship armed with 11-inch guns, but although she utilized replacement battleship tonnage she was, in fact, an armored

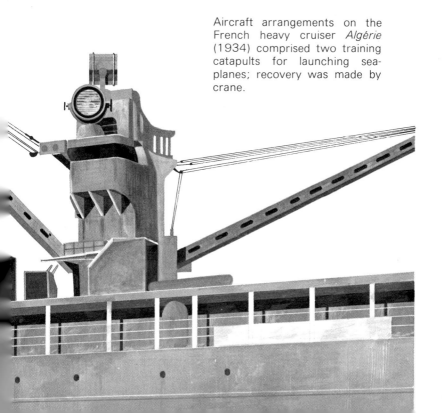

Aircraft arrangements on the French heavy cruiser *Algérie* (1934) comprised two training catapults for launching seaplanes; recovery was made by crane.

cruiser. Armed with six 11-inch and eight 5.9-inch guns and with novel diesel propulsion for a speed of 26 knots, it was claimed that the *Deutschland* could outfight any ship she could not outrun, and, with the exception of a handful of elderly British and Japanese battle cruisers, it was a valid claim. The *Deutschland* so completely outclassed the 8-inch gun cruisers that her appearance ended their construction, except in the United States. Then came the Anglo-German Naval Treaty (1935), under which Germany could build five 8-inch gun cruisers. Germany benefited by the much publicized shortcomings of the earlier vessels of this class that were built by other nations. As the German ships exceeded the tonnage limit by about 3,000 tons they were not surprisingly superior all-round and had exceptionally high steam conditions—over 1,000 lb/in^2.

The flotilla and anti-aircraft cruiser
Despite the upward trend in cruiser construction, the value of the small cruiser was always recognized, providing it could incorporate a useful armament on a small displacement. The

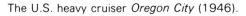

The U.S. heavy cruiser *Oregon City* (1946).

The Dutch flotilla cruiser *Tromp* (1938).

lengths to which this could be taken were shown in the Japanese *Yubari* which, on a displacement of 2,890 tons, had the same broadside as the earlier Japanese 5,000-ton light cruisers. The Dutch *Tromp* was an outstanding example of a cruiser designed to work in support of destroyer flotillas. At 3,787 tons, she had a speed of 34 knots, was armored and mounted six 5.9-inch guns and six 21-inch torpedo tubes.

In 1931 the British Navy converted two old 'C'-class vessels to anti-aircraft ships by replacing their 6-inch guns with ten 4-inch guns, and they were favorably received. This development was taken a stage further by the United States Navy with its *Atlanta* class, which shipped sixteen 5-inch guns in twin turrets. Although the British *Dido* class are often included in this category, they were not specifically

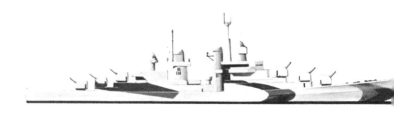

Anti-aircraft cruisers: (*above*) the American *San Juan* and (*below*) the French *De Grasse* (1955), now altered as a command ship.

anti-aircraft cruisers, as their dual-purpose main armament of ten 5.25-inch guns was designed as much for use against surface targets as air targets.

War construction

During World War II, cruisers were used a great deal; there was hardly a major operation in which they were not involved. They were a high priority in those navies which were dependent on sea communications, and Japan's failure to build them proved to be a great mistake. Only the United States embarked on large-scale new construction; most other navies did little more than complete the cruisers they had laid down, or authorized, before the war.

On the whole, the United States Navy built just two types of cruiser at this time: the heavy cruiser with nine 8-inch guns and the light cruiser with twelve 6-inch guns (both had a secondary battery of twelve 5-inch dual-purpose guns). The former ranged from the 13,600-ton *Baltimore* class to the 17,000-ton *Des Moines* class; the latter comprised the

Cleveland and *Fargo* classes of 10,000 tons. In addition there were the 6,000-ton *Oakland* class; modifications of the *Atlanta,* which were enlarged to the 14,700-ton *Worcester* class with twelve 6-inch dual-purpose guns in fully automatic twin turrets; and the large 27,500-ton *Alaska* class with a main armament of nine 12-inch guns.

After the war there was a period of reappraisal owing to the atom bomb, and the gun-armed cruiser became obsolete as, with 16-inch gun battleships supplanted, there was even less need for vessels armed with 8-inch and 6-inch guns. But at least the cruiser passed out of service gracefully; there were no wholesale scrappings, although at the end of their effective lives they were dismantled. The most surprising feature of the postwar years was the large program of cruisers put in operation by the Soviet Union. Of 15,450 tons, the Russian vessels were fast, well protected and armed with twelve 5.9-inch and twelve 3.9-inch guns.

Many hulls left incomplete during and after the war years were later completed in fresh and interesting designs. The

French *De Grasse* finally emerged as an anti-aircraft cruiser and shipped sixteen 5-inch and sixteen 57-millimeter guns in twin turrets at five different levels. Dual-purpose major and secondary guns were the feature of the Dutch and British vessels; the former received eight 6-inch and eight 57-millimeter guns and the latter four 6-inch and six 3-inch guns, all

in twin power-operated turrets. The United States converted most of her cruisers to carry guided missiles and gave them a large array of radar aerials.

The guided-missile cruiser

There are few cruiser characteristics in the current guided-missile cruiser. The name is more one of convenience as the vessels are too large to be satisfactorily classed with frigates and destroyers. The sole American example, the *Long Beach,* is outstanding in that she is nuclear-powered and displaces 14,200 tons. The Italian and Russian vessels of this type are expanded frigate designs, approaching 6,000 tons, built to provide air and anti-submarine defense, but the most recent Italian example—the *Vittorio Veneto*—is of 8,000 tons and incorporates four Polaris long-range ballistic missiles in addition to her defensive guided-missile capability.

A small number of gun-armed cruisers are still retained to lend gunfire support to troops ashore, but it is unlikely that they will be replaced when their service is ended. The cruiser's scouting duties are now undertaken by aircraft and radar.

(*Above*) The American nuclear-powered and missile-armed cruiser *Long Beach* (1961). (*Below*) The British *Seacat* missile system for close air defense.

Her main guns have been outranged by aircraft and missiles, and her trade protection duties are carried out by the frigate. The term cruiser, like destroyer, now merely indicates an approximation of size, and it will probably continue to be applied to large frigates.

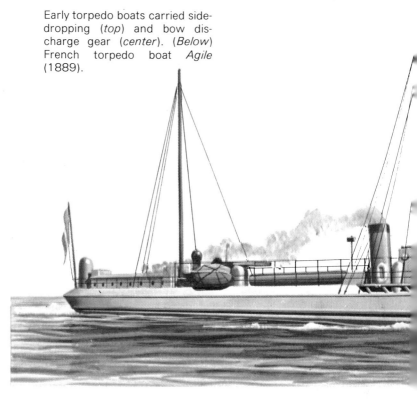

Early torpedo boats carried side-dropping (*top*) and bow discharge gear (*center*). (*Below*) French torpedo boat *Agile* (1889).

TORPEDO BOATS AND DESTROYERS

Torpedo boats and launches

The torpedo has always had the advantage that it could be carried by a small craft. As it was automotive its discharge was a relatively simple matter, yet its power was sufficient to sink, or seriously damage, the largest vessel.

The earliest torpedo boats (about 1875) were as fast as existing machinery permitted. Contemporary mechanical limitations restricted their dimensions in the interest of high speed. Torpedoes were carried on each side in dropping gear that was extended during action, rather like boats under davits. In consequence, it was necessary to aim the boat at the target, and this principle was maintained until fairly recent times, despite later advances with torpedoes and control equipment.

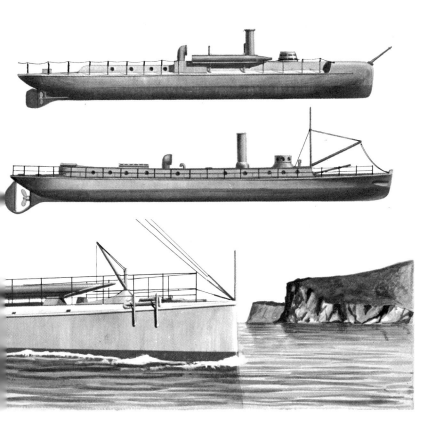

Most of the space in early torpedo craft was taken up by the boilers and reciprocating (piston) machinery, with the conning position (bridge) usually placed well aft. To improve forward vision the funnels were made as slim as possible and, as the only high points available, they carried the steaming lights. Crew accommodations were crude (or non-existent). A shelter, or cabin, was the usual provision for the men during a 12-hour operating period. At first the hull was made of wood for lightness but this was soon replaced by steel.

Naturally, such small, frail craft were very much at the mercy of the weather. However, they could be built in large numbers and located at strategic points around the coast. Thus, they could make a close blockade by enemy naval forces so hazardous that it would soon be discontinued.

The 1st-class torpedo boat

Such was the demand for torpedo boats that their development was very rapid.* Three main types soon emerged:
1st- and 2nd-class torpedo boats and torpedo launches. The
1st-class boats operated independently; the 2nd-class boats,
more restricted in operation, were sized to be hoisted by battleships and cruisers for transport, if necessary; and the smaller
torpedo launches had to be carried by a parent ship to the
scene of operations. The 1st-class boat has survived, with
variations, to the present day, while the 2nd-class boats
and torpedo launches became obsolete before the 1900's.

By about 1880 the 1st-class boat had become long and
narrow. There were generally two conning positions, one
immediately abaft the fo'c'sle, and one aft, with the ma-

chinery arranged amidships and driving twin screws. For
greater accuracy, torpedoes were now launched from a fixed
bow tube (protected by a turtle-backed fo'c'sle) and from
rotatable tubes mounted around the after conning tower.
Normally, 3-pounder guns were mounted on the conning
tower roofs, but heavier 6-pounder guns and machine guns
could be shipped if torpedoes were not carried and then the
craft could be used as a gunboat against enemy torpedo boats.

The torpedo gunboat

One of many defensive counters to early torpedo craft was
the torpedo gunboat, which evolved from the torpedo boat
itself.

---

*For example, between 1874–91 no less than 222 torpedo boats were built
at Chiswick by Thornycroft, British commercial shipbuilders.

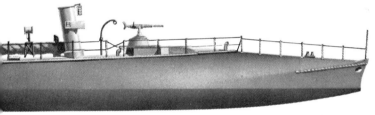

Two examples of later torpedo boats: the German *G .88* of 1898 (*above*) and the Spanish vessel *Arieté,* completed in 1887 (*below*).

The torpedo gunboat (TGB) was larger and more weatherly than the torpedo boat (TB), and carried heavier, more numerous armament. However, the torpedo gunboat was made to look rather ridiculous by later, faster 1st-class torpedo boats.

One reason for the rapid improvement of the 1st-class torpedo boat was that construction was in the hands of specialist private builders who naturally did not like to see their vessels countered by simple defensive measures. The construction of British torpedo gunboats, however, had been allocated to the Royal Dockyards. This provided an added spur to the private builders, who feared losing their monopoly in fast, light warships. It was, perhaps, no coincidence that the only British torpedo gunboat put out to private contract—the *Speedy*—made her designed speed while all others failed to do so.

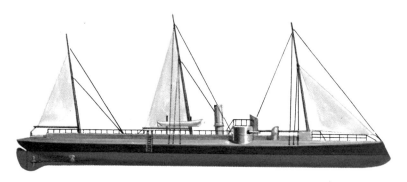

The British torpedo gunboats had the first vertical triple expansion engines installed in warships and took steam at 150 lb/in² from four locomotive boilers. These engines were built to develop 3,000 horsepower at natural draft and 4,000 hp at forced draft for speeds of 19 and 21 knots respectively, but insufficient steam was generated at forced draft so that the designed speed was not attained. The exception was the *Speedy*, which private builders had provided with eight watertube-coil boilers supplying an abundance of steam at 200 lb/in².

(*Above*) The French torpedo gunboat *Bombe* of 1887 and (*below*) the British *Speedy* (1894). Torpedo gunboats were built as the first counter to torpedo boat attack but in practice they were not fast enough to be successful.

One satisfactory feature of the torpedo gunboats was their seaworthiness, and as the weather worsened so their superiority over torpedo boats was made evident. Ironically, the degree of bad weather required for this was usually sufficient to keep torpedo boats in harbor.

The torpedo boat destroyer

Following the failure of the 450-ton torpedo gunboat to catch the 100-ton torpedo boat, British private builders proposed in 1892 that the machinery of the former be installed in an enlarged torpedo boat of about 250 tons to secure the high speed vitally lacking in the gunboat. The idea originated with one of the commercial specialist torpedo boat constructors who shared in the order for six prototype craft. They were called torpedo boat destroyers (TBD's)—later abbreviated to destroyers—and were to steam at 27 knots and have a good gun armament.

The torpedo boat destroyer was similar to, but larger and more seaworthy than, the contemporary torpedo boat; however, as most of the additional space was occupied by machinery there was little in the way of extra comfort for the crew. The armament comprised one 12-pounder gun on the roof of

The French torpedo boat destroyer *Durandal* (1900) possessed the speed that torpedo gunboats lacked.

the conning tower forward, three 6-pounder guns placed on each side abaft the turtle-backed fo'c'sle and one fixed bow tube and two single training tubes for 18-inch torpedoes. The bow tube was later discarded as it was of limited use, and two extra 6-pounder guns were added amidships.

The torpedo boat destroyer emerged as a dual-function vessel which could accompany the fleet and provide it with a craft both sufficiently fast and well-armed to destroy contemporary torpedo boats; it also replaced the latter for delivering torpedo attacks. Although torpedo boats were still built, mainly for minor navies with only coast defense commitments, major navies soon stopped building them altogether.

The ocean-going destroyer

While there was no denying the success of the first torpedo boat destroyers, they were only a little less fragile than the torpedo boats they replaced. However, as they had now become an integral part of the fleet and were as necessary to it as the cruiser screen, it was essential that their seaworthiness be improved so that they could keep station with the fleet in all weathers.

About 1900, a marked feature of the ocean-going destroyers that followed the turtle-backed torpedo boat destroyers was a more robust hull, heavier scantlings and a short, raised fo'c'sle, giving improved seaworthiness besides extra crew space. The conning tower in earlier torpedo boat destroyers had proved of little use as it was too low and vision from it was very limited. In fact, the 12-pounder gun

platform over it was more frequently used as a bridge when at sea. Although the conning tower was still present in some of the new destroyers, it was backed by a chart room and a radio shack over which was a substantial open bridge that could comfortably accommodate and shelter the sea watch.

As a result of these improvements displacement tonnage was doubled. Although speed was therefore nominally less in smooth water, this was not much of a practical disadvantage, as the earlier torpedo boat destroyers rapidly lost speed in rough weather. Initially there was no increase in armament, but later destroyers sacrificed the 6-pounder guns for extra 12-pounders. Early models, such as the British *River* class, were criticized

by strategists because they were larger, slower and no better armed than their predecessors, but there was no complaint from seamen. Destroyer officers were well aware of the less obvious advantages of greater reliability, less maintenance and reduced discomfort for the crew.

The turbine destroyer

The introduction of the steam turbine was a major step in destroyer development. All early turbine experimental work was undertaken in destroyers and only much later was the machinery extended to cruisers and battleships. Turbines offered economies in weight and space and naturally lent themselves to fast, light warships, but their high fuel consumption and high rate of revolution presented difficulties.

As early as 1900 experimental turbine destroyers were

Ocean-going destroyers: the British *Eden* of 1903 (*above*) and the American *Bainbridge* of 1902 (*below*).

reaching 35 knots with 10,000 horsepower. This speed did not improve much over the next 50 years. The much larger power output, however, required more steam. Thus, economies in weight and space were offset by more boilers. As the boilers were still coal-fired, a larger engine room crew proved necessary. The high revolutions per minute (rpm) of direct coupled turbines led to some odd screw arrangements. Propeller diameter had to be kept small and required multiple screws on each shaft. A reciprocating engine for long-distance cruising was proposed to extend the radius of action. All these setbacks were overcome by the provision of lower-rpm cruising turbines and reduction gearing scaled for greater fuel economy. Later, oil-firing substantially reduced the engine room crew as coal no longer need be shoveled.

By the beginning of World War I the destroyer had nearly 1,000 tons displacement. It was powered by direct coupled turbines of 25,000 hp at 34 knots, taking steam at 250 lb/in² from three oil-fired boilers. It was armed with three 4-inch guns and two twin 21-inch torpedo tubes and could accompany the fleet practically anywhere. Two significant advances were made during the war: reduction gearing (installed experimentally prewar) and superimposed guns.

The superimposition of guns
Most destroyers mounted guns forward, amidships and aft. While all could bear on the broadside, there were wide arcs over bow and stern covered only by a single gun.

In 1916 the British Navy took the step with its 'V' and 'W' destroyer classes of shipping two guns forward and aft and superimposing them American-style (see page 20). This disposition had not yet been extended by any nation to destroyers as additional top weight was thought to impair stability. This proved not to be the case with the 'V's and 'W's and they were almost universally copied. For the next 30 years this arrangement remained a standard layout and it is a striking example of the basic simplicity underlying every good design.

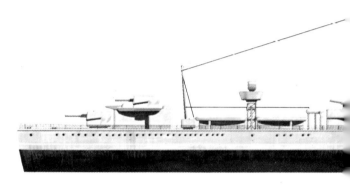

The WWI motor torpedo boat

In order to skim over defensive minefields and attack enemy ships in their bases, the British Navy proposed in 1916 a shallow-draft launch not to exceed $4\frac{1}{4}$ tons in weight — so that it could be hoisted on a cruiser's davits. With a speed of about 30 knots, it would be armed with an 18-inch torpedo. A private builder, applying their experience with racing hydroplanes,* built the craft. The weights for a typical boat were: hull $2\frac{1}{4}$ tons, machinery $\frac{3}{4}$ ton and load (equipment, armament, fuel, etc.) 1 ton. Powered by a non-reversible 12-cylinder gasoline engine of 250 hp, the 40-foot boats attained 33 or 34 knots and launched their torpedoes tail-first over the stern.

*It is interesting to recall the first British Navy torpedo boat, the *Lightning,* was developed from the steam launch *Miranda* in 1871; and that another *Miranda* (IV), a hydroplane built in 1910, was the basis for coastal motor boat development.

Subsequent British motor torpedo boats were lengthened to 55 feet, then 70 feet, and the weight limitation had to be abandoned. The 55-foot boat had twin screws. Depending on the type of gasoline engines installed, it made between 32 and 40 knots. It was armed with two torpedoes and four depth charges. The 70-foot boats were minelayers and could carry four 1-ton mines, but they made only 28½ knots (except one boat fitted with 24-cylinder gasoline engines which made over 40 knots).

Similar triple screw boats were built in Germany and

Contemporary destroyer designs at the close of World War I: the British 'V' class (*above*) and the American *Wickes* class (*below*).

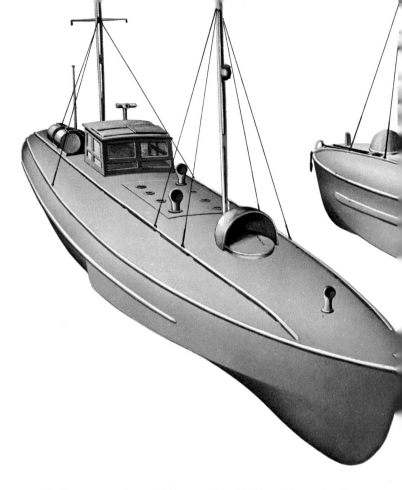

carried one torpedo at 30 knots. The Italian Navy also began
a large series of coastal motor boats which could be armed
either as minelayers (four mines), torpedo boats (two torpedoes in side-dropping gear), or gunboats (one 3-pounder
and machine guns) but were slower at 24 knots. One of these
boats, *MAS.15* (Rizzo), succeeded in sinking the Austro-
Hungarian battleship *Szent Istvan* in 1917 and made her
escape despite the presence of 30-knot enemy destroyers.

The large destroyer
The practice of providing each destroyer flotilla with a more
powerfully armed leader of greater size dated back to the time
of the first ocean-going destroyers that could accompany the
fleet. From this came the idea of forming flotillas solely of

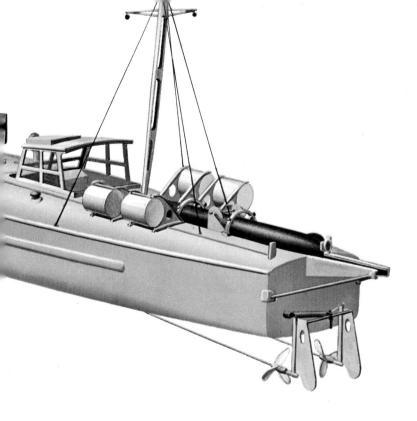

British 55-foot coastal motor boats of World War I. Torpedoes were carried aft in a trough and were launched tail-first over the stern.

heavy destroyers to provide a concentration of force that could overwhelm all flotilla opposition. As such destroyers were expensive they were not initially built in large numbers. Moreover, they demonstrated the old tactic of an inferior fleet seeking to make up for small numbers with superior vessels. Thus, during World War I, the Germany Navy produced large destroyers armed with four 5.9-inch guns, but they were not outstandingly successful. Too much armament had been crowded onto a hull of too little displacement.

The smaller navies—such as those of Argentina, Spain, Yugoslavia and Poland—had some similar heavy destroyer units built. The Argentine and Spanish destroyers were based on British *Shakespeare*-class ships and displaced

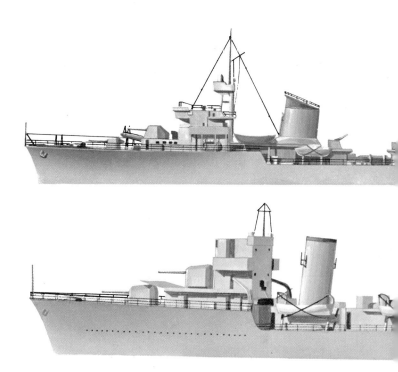

1,500 tons. Capable of 36 knots, they were armed with five 4.7-inch guns and six 21-inch torpedo tubes. The Yugoslav *Dubrovnik,* at 1,880 tons, was capable of 37 knots and was armed with four 5.5-inch guns and six torpedo tubes. The Polish *Blyskawica* and *Grom,* 1,975 tons, did 39 knots, and were armed with seven 4.7-inch guns and six torpedo tubes.

After World War I the French Navy started on a large program of heavy destroyers (the *contre-torpilleurs*). These vessels had developed from the 1,500-ton type of 1922, armed with four 5.1-inch guns and six 21.7-inch torpedo tubes and capable of 33 knots, to the 2,930-ton type of 1934, armed with eight 5.5-inch guns and ten 21.7-inch torpedo tubes and steaming at 39 knots.

As the first London Naval Treaty (1930) had imposed a total tonnage on destroyers, most major navies—the French being a singular exception—were inclined to spread this tonnage over more numerous destroyers of the standard type. All nations, however, built small groups of heavy destroyers. Thus, the Italian Navy built two series of heavy units of about 1,600 tons (six or eight 4.7-inch guns); the British

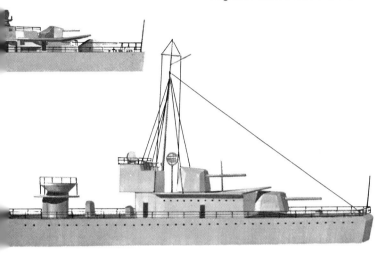

Two large destroyers, both British-built: (*above*) the Polish *Grom* (1936) and (*below*) the Yugoslav *Dubrovnik* (1932).

Navy, the *Tribal* class of 1,870 tons (eight 4.7-inch guns); and the United States Navy, the *Porter* class of 1,850 tons (eight 5-inch guns).

For a while Japan had followed a similar policy, but in 1925 she started the *Fubuki* class of 1,700 tons (actually of over 2,000 tons) and 34 knots, which were armed with six 5-inch guns and nine torpedo tubes. The latter were thought to be for standard 21-inch torpedoes, but much later it was found that they were for the greatly improved 24-inch torpedoes used with such telling effect during World War II. When the German Navy embarked on destroyer construction in 1934 it also turned to heavy units for its small flotilla, and its 1,600-ton (actually over 2,200-ton) vessels carried five 5-inch guns and eight 21-inch torpedo tubes which, like the Japanese units, were provided with reloads.

The modern motor torpedo boat
Between the wars relatively few coastal motor boats were built. However, from about 1935 on, Germany, Italy and Great Britain showed fresh interest in the design.

To its great advantage, the Germany Navy possessed a lightweight diesel engine system and was able to build robust round-bottomed craft of little over a hundred tons, capable of 35 knots and of carrying four torpedoes. The stepped hull of limited seaworthiness was preferred by the Italian Navy and, at 24 tons, it could carry two torpedoes at 42 knots. For improved seaworthiness the British abandoned the stepped coastal motor boat and built a spined hull of 22 tons displacement, 33 knots, and with two torpedoes. In the United Kingdom there was a marked rivalry between two commercial firms, British Power Boat and Vosper. Although the latter eventually secured the Admiralty contract for motor torpedo boats (MTB), the former brought their craft to the United States. The United States Navy accepted the design as the prototype for the American patrol torpedo (PT) boat that saw heavy service in the Pacific theater of war.

Standard British 70-foot motor torpedo boat in service at the outbreak of World War II with fixed deck tubes for launching torpedoes.

All these boats were of wood construction. Except for Germany's diesels, they were powered by high-octane gasoline engines; they were therefore very prone to fire and explosion. Although more seaworthy than the older coastal motor boat, the motor torpedo boat was still hampered by rough weather. Its presence was usually revealed by its unsilenced engines; later a separate low-powered engine was provided for silent attack, but its low speed proved impractical.

War construction
After the outbreak of World War II, destroyer construction was given a high priority in all navies. The British Navy immediately reverted to the standard type to speed production, and a feature of all war designs was a marked increase in anti-aircraft fire. The German Navy continued with its heavy destroyers and for a short period substituted 5.9-inch for 5-inch guns. It planned some interesting projects with diesel main propulsion but none was ever completed.

French construction came to a halt after the surrender in 1940. The Italian Navy pursued a line similar to that of Britain. Japan progressed vigorously with a rather heavy standard destroyer even though, like Germany, she would have been better served by a larger number of smaller units.

However, the increased destroyer construction of other navies was overshadowed by the United States' effort. U.S. production switched to two large standard designs. The earlier *Fletcher* class of 2,050 tons made 37 knots and were armed with five 5-inch guns and ten 21-inch torpedo tubes,

while the later *Sumner* and *Gearing* classes ran to 2,200 and 2,425 tons, 36½ knots, and were armed with six 5-inch guns and ten torpedo tubes. No less than 410 destroyers of these classes were authorized, although the end of the war caused sixty cancellations.

The destroyer escort
Although it was not the most suitable vessel for anti-submarine and anti-aircraft escort duties, the destroyer was used for this purpose because it was the only type of vessel available in large numbers. However, even before the war the United States and British navies had already decided that a destroyer used for escort duties could be smaller, slower and less complex than the fleet unit. It could therefore be produced more rapidly and at less cost. Consequently, the prewar program was continued until 1942 when even simpler frigates were put into production. The Japanese came to the same conclusion as the United States, but not until 1943, after suffering heavy losses to its fleet destroyers.

These pictures show how funnels, once the epitome of speed, have gradually decreased in number. (*From the left, top to bottom*) American *Wickes* class of 1916 with four funnels; a French *Jaguar* class of 1924 (three funnels); a British 'G' class with two (1936), and an Italian *Oriani* class (1937) with one funnel.

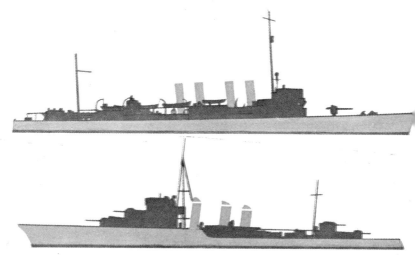

The three designs were in no way similar: the British units were small destroyers; the American vessels had a distinctive profile, the slower units fitted with diesel-electric, and the faster units turbo-electric, propulsion; the Japanese vessels had severe utility lines similar to their sloops.

Both the German and Italian navies had built torpedo boats* before the war, and they continued to build them during the war as a type of small destroyer. The torpedo boat, however, while smaller and cheaper than the destroyer, and possessing many of its refinements, lacked the destroyer escort's essential simplicity, an important factor in production.

The fast patrol boat
Developments in many fields enabled light naval craft to become very effective small fighting units in the postwar years. The gas turbine gave high speed from a compact and lightweight power unit, and as an alternative there was the lightweight diesel engine. In addition, a wide selection of light, compact and highly reliable weaponry and detection and electronic systems became available so that light naval craft could be armed and equipped for specialist roles.

*Both navies were limited to 600 tons for these vessels by treaty: the German Navy under the Versailles Treaty and the Italian Navy under the London Naval Treaty which placed no limitation on vessels of 600 tons and under.

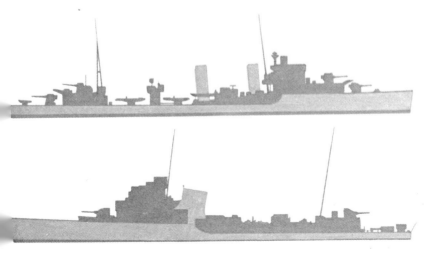

Gas turbine-powered torpedo boats: the Swedish *Spica* (*above*) of 1966; (*below*) the *Brave Swordsman,* a British vessel (1958).

During World War II, coastal forces included motor torpedo boats, motor gunboats and a variety of other motor launches. They were classed as fast patrol boats of three main types:
(a) the steel round-bottomed gunboat powered by either gas turbines or diesel engines;
(b) the wooden hard-keeled convertible torpedo boat/gunboat/minelayer/raiding craft with high-speed gas turbines;
(c) the steel round-bottomed patrol boat with diesel propulsion and a large radius of action.

As the gas turbine has a higher fuel consumption than the diesel engine, the choice between them for high-speed craft is determined by the radius of action required. Beyond a certain point it is more economic to install the heavier diesel engine with lower fuel consumption. Round-bottomed craft are now fitted with fin stabilization to make them more seaworthy than their wartime counterparts. Fin stabilization and gas turbines have widened the scope of fast patrol boats so considerably that the present-day 100-ton craft have a greater capability than 1,000-ton prewar vessels.

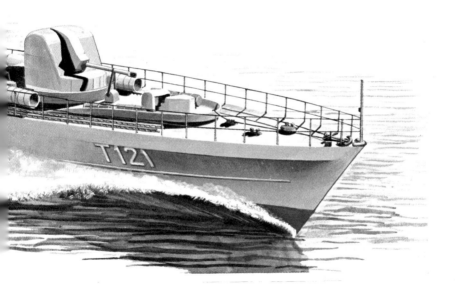

Gun-armed destroyers such as the Soviet *Skory*-class vessel (*above*) of 1949 have now been supplemented by missile-armed destroyer.s; an example is the American *Charles F. Adams* class (*below*) dating from 1960.

The missile destroyer

As a type, the destroyer, like the cruiser, has undergone a metamorphosis in the years since World War II. The current missile destroyer is a missile-armed vessel of destroyer size. If it was larger, or smaller, it would be loosely called a missile cruiser or missile frigate. An anomaly arises here as the United States Navy realistically rates frigates above destroyers, while vessels below destroyer size are classed as escorts and were developed from the destroyer escort.

Only the Soviet Union built large numbers of conventional destroyers after the war. They were fine examples of their type and politically they have served the Soviet Navy well, helping to extend Russia's influence into the Mediterranean Sea.

Most missile destroyers have a combined main propulsion plant comprising long-life steam turbines for cruising and gas turbines for high speed; moreover, the gas turbine can be brought rapidly into use from the shut-down condition. The missile armament usually includes both long-range and short-range anti-aircraft missiles. It is supplemented by a gun system for bombardment purposes and an anti-submarine force, including a helicopter. This armament is accompanied by extensive radar installations.

Considerable space is taken up by computers and other

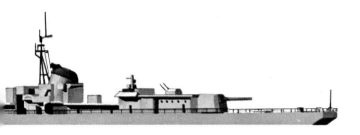

electronic gear associated with the missile systems, as well as by the communications equipment required for modern warships. Therefore, there is a heavy demand for electricity. A typical missile destroyer's generating capacity consists of two 1,000-kilowatt alternators (powered by steam turbines), two 500-kilowatt alternators (powered by gas turbines) and a 750-kilowatt emergency set, also powered by a gas turbine. In areas contaminated with nuclear fall-out, the crew can withdraw into the gas-tight citadel which is supplied with filtered air, from which the main machinery can be kept under remote control.

A 1902 submarine of the American Holland-type, running on the surface.

SUBMARINES

The Holland Submarine

The submarine began as a craft that could submerge to avoid detection when attacking. However, early submarines were ahead of their time; there were not yet effective means of underwater propulsion and navigation, nor were suitable weapons available. Early submarines were therefore small and manually propelled. The first method of attack was to approach, while submerged, an anchored warship and attach an explosive charge to its hull.

Only after the internal combustion engine had become available for surface propulsion did the submarine develop into an effective combatant vessel. A system of storage batteries, charged off the surface propulsion engines, provided the electric power for underwater propulsion. Finally came the torpedo, the periscope and the gyrocompass. Before this, submarines had all lacked one, or more, of the essential features mentioned above, and their effectiveness was therefore limited.

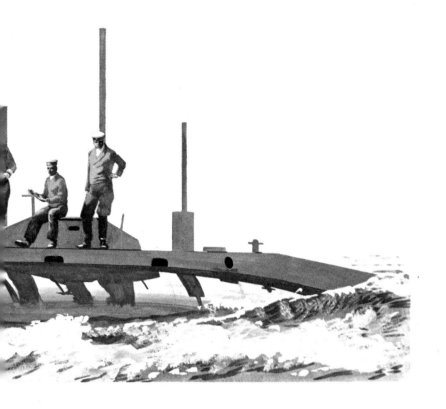

For this reason the American designer J. B. Holland's submarine of 1900 is generally considered the earliest effective craft of this type. Many foreign navies—including those of Austria-Hungary, Great Britain, Italy, Japan and Russia— adopted the Holland design for their own first submarines. The first Holland boat for the United States Navy was a coast defense unit of limited radius which displaced only 120 tons submerged. The cylindrical hull was of full form and was divided into three main compartments: the torpedo room forward, the control room amidships, and the engine room aft. The two forward compartments were further divided by a deck to provide tank and battery spaces below. A small conning tower was fitted amidships, and, forward of it, was the externally mounted magnetic compass. When attacking, the boat had to break surface at intervals so that the target could be kept under observation because the vessel ran blind when submerged. The British fitted a periscope to the Holland submarine, thereby enabling the target to be tracked while

submerged. Main propulsion came from a 160 hp gasoline engine and a 70 hp electric motor (which the fully-charged batteries could supply for four hours). The armament comprised a fixed bow tube for 14-inch torpedoes, and two or four reloads were carried internally. There was little in the way of comfort for the crew of seven, but this was acceptable because of the boat's limited radius of operation.

Developments up to 1914

Before the outbreak of World War I, submarine development was rapid. Succeeding classes increased in size and scope of employment. Not even the battlefleet at sea was considered safe from submarine attack. Indeed, having survived the threat of surface torpedo attack, the capital ship was now confronted with the same attack from an unseen assailant. The control of areas of strategic importance, such as the North Sea and the Mediterranean, was abruptly placed in dispute from the time battleships were confronted by submarines.

Although Germany at first lagged behind other major navies in adopting submarines, she introduced the use of the heavy oil, and then the diesel, engine, which completely replaced gasoline motors for surface propulsion. Besides eliminating the danger of explosion prevalent with gasoline vapor, the higher output and greater fuel economy of the diesel engine advanced the submarine to an ocean-going craft. This placed further restrictions on major surface units. Thus, by the outbreak of war, submarines had reached the dimensions and performance summarized in Table 1 on page 126.

However, the above comparisons tend to be misleading. Not all navies had reached the same stage in submarine development. Neither did all the boats listed achieve designed performance. It is worth noting that all boats shipped one or more deck guns with the exception of the Russian craft, which shipped external launching gear for torpedoes on deck.

(*Opposite*) British 'D'-class submarine (1910). (*Above*) 'K'-
class fleet submarine (1917).

Submarine warfare 1914–18

An unproven weapon at the start of World War I, the submarine quickly established its prowess in September of 1914, when the German sub U-9 sank three British armored cruisers singlehandedly off the Dutch coast. Thereafter the Germans used subs against merchant shipping, and the Allies found themselves in grave danger. By 1917, the Allied situation was so serious that—with great armies locked in stalemate on the European continent—the U-boat almost decided the entire war in favor of Germany. Finally, though, the convoy system, in combination with new anti-submarine countermeasures, was evolved by the Allies, reducing the high losses in shipping. Nonetheless, from 1914 to 1918, German submarines destroyed some 2,500 Allied merchant ships, totaling nearly 12 million tons.

Prior to the war, Germany had completed 45 U-boats. During the war years, the German Navy embarked on a crash construction program, with the aim of putting into service 766 new submarines. By the war's end, 347 had been completed. Germany's submarines fell into four main classes: seagoing U-boats; UB and UF boats, which operated in coastal waters; specially fitted U-boats and UC-boats that operated as minelayers on the high seas and in coastal waters; and submarine cruisers.

The submarine cruiser's main armament was the gun, which it surfaced to employ against unescorted merchant vessels. For a time, this undersea 'cruiser,' with its battery of twin 5.9-inch guns, was the most feared threat to mercantile shipping. But the use of well-armed escort vessels in the convoy system eventually diminished the submarine cruiser's effect.

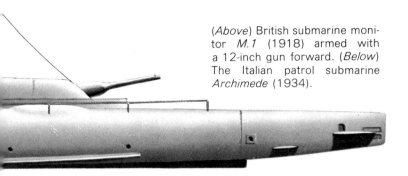

(*Above*) British submarine monitor *M.1* (1918) armed with a 12-inch gun forward. (*Below*) The Italian patrol submarine *Archimede* (1934).

Britain's steam submarine

Exaggerated reports of the high surface speed of German submarines made the British Admiralty believe that the German Navy possessed fleet submarines. Submarines able to travel in company with the surface fleet — submerging to go into action on engaging the enemy's fleet warships — would pose a serious peril to the navy of any nation. Britain elected to construct submarines with high-speed surface propulsion to operate with the English fleet. Such craft would have to be capable of sustained cruising speeds of 21 knots. Britain's diesel-powered 'J'-class submarines couldn't make this speed and there seemed no alternative but to build a fleet submarine whose surface propulsion would be provided by the steam turbine.

Thus, the British Admiralty undertook the surprising — and apparently retrogressive step — of reintroducing steam in the submarine. The resultant 'K' class, displacing 2,650 tons submerged and 338 feet long, was driven by geared steam-turbines developing 10,000 horsepower for a surface speed of 24 knots. A superstructure amidships supported a small wheelhouse and two hinged funnels. At each end of the superstructure were 4-inch guns. Between the wheelhouse and fore funnel was

mounted a 3-inch anti-aircraft gun. The ten 18-inch torpedo tubes were disposed four forward, four amidships and two in the superstructure.

Auxiliary surface propulsion was by an 800 hp diesel generator supplying power to the electric motors; these enabled the steam plant to be shut and diving accomplished more rapidly given early warning of an enemy approach.

In all, twenty-seven units were ordered. They had an unhappy history. One—later salvaged—sank during trials. Six were lost by accident. Five were cancelled. Four were converted into submarine monitors. The remainder ultimately were scrapped. Their least satisfactory features were their clumsiness when submerged and the length of time they required to dive (however, they easily made their speed on the surface and were reasonably seaworthy given careful handling). Ironically, the close of the war revealed that the German Navy possessed no fleet submarines; nor had it planned any.

The submarine monitor
As the submarine generally had to close to within 1,000 yards to secure a hit with the torpedo and was frequently unable to do so owing to target movement and its own low speed when submerged, the Germans armed their submarine cruisers with a heavy gun that made it possible to engage targets at a considerably greater range.

The British decided to do likewise, employing a much heavier gun. Four uncompleted vessels of the 'K' class—*K. 18–21*

which were renumbered as *M.1–4*—were selected for this purpose and were armed with 12-inch guns removed from old battleships. These could be laid and trained through 20 degrees, but could be loaded only on the surface. The vessels were powered by diesel engines. They retained torpedo armament fitted in the bows.

They passed through their trials satisfactorily and the 12-inch gun presented no difficulties. The British Admiralty, however, feared that Germany, in turn, might adopt the submarine monitor's heavier guns if so prompted. Consequently, construction was slowed down and the least advanced models were cancelled. Only one submarine monitor was completed before the end of hostilities, and this one was sent by Britain to the Mediterranean away from German eyes.

The patrol submarine

After World War I, most navies concentrated on the construction of sea-going patrol submarines based on such successful and war-proven craft as the medium-sized British 'L' and German 'U.81' classes.

More attention was given to submarine qualities such as rapid diving, good torpedo armament, the provision of reloads and increased underwater radius; to good surface qualities which would maintain an adequate sustained speed; and to more reliable equipment. So, while performance was not spectacular, overall capability improved significantly.

The German coastal submarine *U.9* (1936).

Patrol submarines ranged between 1,000 and 1,500 tons and made 16 to 18 knots on the surface. Generally they were armed with one 4-inch or 4.7-inch gun, four or six bow tubes and two stern torpedo tubes. The French and Netherlands navies both preferred to carry most of the torpedo tubes externally in trainable mountings that could be aimed individually. The more usual practice was to fit tubes internally where they could be reloaded more readily. During the 1930's, however, many submarines added fixed external tubes to increase their attacking power. The British 'T' class, for example, were provided with eleven torpedo tubes, of which five were fitted externally. In diving, sea water was admitted as ballast, usually into saddle tanks from which it could be expelled on surfacing. The conning tower was sited about amidships. Stout jumper wires ran from the stem and stern to the periscope standard so that any underwater obstructions rode over the gun(s) and conning tower.

Although American and Japanese patrol submarines were invariably larger than their European counterparts, Japan also built smaller patrol craft of under 1,000 tons for work in narrow seas. Coastal boats of about 250 tons were built only by those navies with specific requirements for them.

The submarine cruiser

After World War I, the United States Navy and the Japanese Navy both demonstrated interest in submarine cruisers because of the performance of the German wartime 'U.131' and 'U.139' classes. Japan continued to build this type right up to and through World War II. The United States, however, soon abandoned the design and started fresh development with smaller patrol submarines. Brief details of some American and Japanese submarine cruisers are given in Table 2 on page 127.

Great Britain and France also built a few submarine cruisers but did not continue this type. The French *Surcouf* was particularly interesting. The vessel had a submerged displacement of 4,304 tons and a surface speed of 18½ knots. She was armed with two 8-inch guns in a twin turret and eight 21.7-inch and four 15.7-inch torpedo tubes. She also carried a seaplane and a light boarding boat (this was later removed). The British *X.1* was more conventional. She displaced 3,600 tons submerged, could make 19½ knots on the surface and was armed with four 5.2-inch guns in twin turrets and six 21-inch torpedo tubes. Although both Britain and France possessed numerous overseas bases, neither of them envisaged a

The German patrol submarine *U.26* (1936).

The first nuclear-powered submarine, America's *Nautilus* (1955), which passed beneath the North Pole on August 3, 1958.

large-scale war involving mercantile interests, and the submarine cruiser—which was costly to build—was not a high priority.

For Japan, planning to challenge the United States for control of the Pacific, the large submarine appeared strategically important. The Japanese Navy embarked on a series of large submarines which were designed to act as command centers

for its scouting and raiding squadrons. The 'I.400' class had a radius of 30,000 miles at 16½ knots and surpassed even the *Surcouf* in size. On deck was a large hangar able to accommodate three torpedo/bomber aircraft with a catapult arranged along the foredeck; the conning tower was offset to port over the hangar.

The minelaying submarine

During World War I the submarine showed that it was able to operate in enemy-controlled waters. This suggested its use in infiltrating enemy shipping routes, coasts and harbors and acting as a minelayer. The shallow waters of the North Sea — and the continental shelf generally — were very suitable for mining, and the German Navy was first in the field with its small minelayers (or UC-boats); these undertook lays all

(*Above*) The British submarine cruiser *X.1* (1926). (*Below*) The French submarine cruiser *Surcouf* (1932).

around the United Kingdom coast and could work well inshore. The first UC-boats entered service in mid-1915 and, displacing only 183 tons submerged, they carried 12 mines in six mine shafts forward. Nearly 200 of these craft were projected during the war, of which more than half were put

into service. The final models displaced 564 tons submerged and were armed with one 3.5-inch or 4.1-inch gun and three 19.7-inch torpedo tubes besides stowing 14 mines.

The British effort came later and was much smaller. Actually, no special minelaying submarines were built during the war by Britain. Initially, special mines were developed which submarines could discharge through the standard torpedo tube. In 1916, external mine shafts were provided in six 'E'-class submarines.

Between the wars most navies built small classes of minelaying submarines. The German Navy developed a special mine to fit the standard 21-inch submarine torpedo tube so that virtually any of its boats could be used for minelaying when needed. Submarine mining was not so intensive during World War II as anticipated, partly because aircraft could take over this mission. Minelaying submarines generally carried their mines in free-flooding release shafts, fitted either externally or internally.

The 'true' submarine

In actual fact the submarine was misnamed. The craft would have been more correctly described by the word 'submersible'—meaning a craft that can submerge but spends most of its time on the surface.

During World War II, Germany mounted a submarine campaign against mercantile shipping on a scale far surpass-

ing that of World War I. To some extent the U-boat was countered by the Allies with much improved anti-submarine countermeasures, supplemented by aircraft. What finally tipped the balance in favor of the anti-submarine forces, however, was the fitting of search radar in airplanes (it had already been installed in ships). Thus, planes were no longer dependent on visual sightings and could press home attacks by day or night, in clear weather or reduced visibility.

To survive, the submarine had to remain submerged for far longer periods than were possible with its conventional, battery-driven electric motors. The long-term answer lay in developing a suitable closed-cycle engine that did not require air. In the interim, however, Germany introduced two short-term measures: the *schnorchel,* or air mast, about 30 feet in height, through which air could be drawn to supply the main diesel engines while the submarine ran submerged at shallow depths; and greatly increased battery capacity for longer running-time at steep depths. Later models had both the *schnorchel* (snorkel) and larger batteries. When cruising submerged at *schnorchel* depths, the diesel engines drove gener-

ators that supplied the electric motors. Below *schnorchel* depths, the diesel machinery was shut down and the power for the electric motors came from the batteries. As the craft was designed to carry out a patrol completely submerged, all surface performance characteristics could be dropped and the hull shaped for optimum underwater performance. This slim, streamlined, deep hull, with a figure-of-eight cross-section, was first in a new generation of 'true' submarines.

The resulting type XXI submarine had a submerged displacement of 1,819 tons, a submerged speed of 16 knots and was armed with six 21-inch torpedo tubes and 17 reloads. It was silent running, hard to detect and consequently difficult to destroy, but it was put into production too late to halt the German slide to defeat.

Despite intensive effort the German Navy was not successful in producing a closed-cycle engine, but it came close to it with the Walter system, whereby the thermal energy produced by the decomposition of a high concentration of hydrogen peroxide was sufficient to turn a turbine. Although a large number of Walter boats were planned, only a few actually

(*Above*) The Dutch minelaying submarine *O.19* (1939). (*Below*) The German submarine *U.793* (1944).

The U.S. nuclear-powered hunter-killer submarine *Whale* (1968).

entered service. Allied postwar experimental craft were only a bit more successful.

The midget submarine

Midget subs were built for special operations, such as infiltrating enemy harbors undetected for surprise attacks. The origin of this type of attack craft was to be found in the Italian Navy's World-War-I *Grillo,* a sort of marine tank.

Before World War II, both the Italian and Japanese navies undertook the construction of midget subs. Because the tiny subs could not cruise for long distances under their own power, they had to be transported to the scene of operations by parent craft. In 1942, after the outbreak of war, Great Britain started a series of midget submersibles. British strategists intended to use the small subs for attacks on the German warships that lay in the fjords of Norway, from where they threatened Allied Atlantic and Arctic convoy routes. Whereas both the Italian and Japanese subs were carried on deck by a parent submarine and were armed with torpedo tubes, Britain's midget sub was towed to the vicinity of operations and armed with explosive charges that were attached to the target ship's hull by frogmen. (Later, Italy's craft were altered in imitation of Britain's.)

In 1944, with D-Day imminent, Germany began building a large series of midget craft to attack Allied invasion fleets. As originally planned, the German midgets would have borne a single mine; however, their armament was changed over to torpedoes that were carried slung underneath the belly.

In addition, all navies had developed various types of 'manned torpedoes.' The British and Italian types had a detachable warhead that was secured to the target's hull, whereas the German and Japanese types were used as conventional torpedoes. No means of escape was provided for the pilot in the Japanese models, whose mission was suicide.

The nuclear submarine

On January 17, 1955, the signal lamp on the American submarine *Nautilus* flashed the following message: 'Under way on nuclear power.' Thus, only a decade after the advent of the atomic age, this new source of power was harnessed and controlled for ship propulsion.

Although the German type XXI boats (p. 121) had come as close to the true submarine as conventional propulsion allowed, America's *Nautilus* can operate completely divorced from the atmosphere. Her closed-cycle nuclear plant gives her a practically unlimited radius of action, while the air in the boat is kept fresh by being continually circulated through a regenerative plant equipped with an oxygen supply and filters. In case of a power failure there is an auxiliary propulsion plant—a back-up system dubbed 'belt-and-braces' in the United States Navy—comprising an electric motor drawing power from either a small bank of batteries or a diesel generator set; an air mast is provided for the generator.

The American Polaris-missile submarine *Francis Scott Key* (1966).

Now truly a vehicle of the deep, the nuclear-powered submarine fully adopted the hull form best suited to totally submerged operation: a streamlined fin was fitted to enclose the periscope standards, masts for radar, radio communications, and position-fixing, and the snorkel. The nuclear submarine actually need break the surface of the water only periodically with its radio mast to receive messages that fix her position. With all surface-performance characteristics eliminated, the best propulsion is obtained by a single large diameter screw turning at low revolutions, with steering rudders placed above and below it.

The missile submarine
The nuclear-powered submarine has come to play an important part in intercontinental ballistic missile systems because

its mobility and elusiveness make it far harder for the foe to destroy than the fixed missile sites ashore.

Although fitted with conventional torpedo tubes, the American Polaris submarine differs fundamentally from past subs in that it is designed almost exclusively to deliver an attack with its 16 missiles on strategic enemy points up to 2,500 miles away; with the substitution of Poseidon missiles, its range is now being extended to 3,500 miles.

At present, the missile submarine represents the ultimate deterrent. Impervious to satellite surveillance, it does remain partly dependent on communications that may betray its presence to hunter-killer submarines. However, an inertial guidance system (gyrocompass) has largely supplanted methods of position-fixing that require surfacing, and its ability to pass beneath the polar ice cap adds to its general elusiveness.

(*Above*) The nuclear-powered and missile-armed French submarine *Redoutable* (1969). (*Below*) Conning tower and gun armament of the Italian patrol submarine *Barbarigo* (1938).

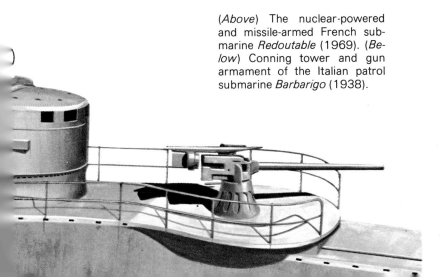

A Japanese '1.400'-class submarine cruiser (1940).

Table 1: submarine development by 1914 (see page 108)

CLASS	DISPLACE-MENT	HORSEPOWER & SPEED	ARMAMENT Guns	TTs•
U.VII Austro-Hungarian	810/930 tons	hp 2,300* hp 1,260† = 16*/10½† knots	1 × 4.1 in.	5 × 17.7 in.
Diane French	630/945 tons	hp 1,800* hp (unknown) = 18½*/11† knots	4 × 65 mm.	10 × 17.7 in.
U.19 German	650/837 tons	hp 1,700* hp 1,200† = 15*/9½† knots	1 × 3.5 in.	4 × 19.7 in.
E British	725/810 tons	hp 1,600* hp 840† = 16*/10† knots	1 × 12 pdr.	5 × 18 in.
Balilla Italian	728/875 tons	hp 1,300* hp 450† = 14*/9† knots	2 × 3 in.	4 × 17.7 in.
I.16 Japanese	520/900 tons	hp 2,100* hp 1,000† = 17½*/9† knots	1 × 3 in.	6 × 18 in.
Nerpa Russian	630/758 tons	hp 500* hp 900† = 11*/9† knots	12 × 17.7 in. 4 internal 8 external	
L American	450/548 tons	hp 900* hp 680† = 14*/10½† knots	1 × 3 in.	4 × 18 in.

*surfaced   †submerged   •torpedo tubes

Table 2: submarine cruisers (see page 115)

CLASS	DISPLACE-MENT†	HORSEPOWER & SPEED	ARMAMENT Guns TTs•		Aircraft	Mines
I.51 (1921) Japanese	2,430 tons	hp 5,200* hp 2,000† = 20*/10† knots	1 × 4.7 in. 1 × 3 in.	8 × 21 in.	—	—
I.1 (1924) Japanese	2,791 tons	hp 6,000* hp 2,600† = 18*/8† knots	2 × 5.5 in.	6 × 21 in.	—	—
I.13 (1944) Japanese	4,762 tons	hp 4,400* hp 1,200† = 16½*/5½† knots	1 × 5.5 in.	6 × 21 in.	2	—
I.400 (1944) Japanese	6,560 tons	hp 7,200* hp 2,400† = 18*/6½† knots	1 × 5.5 in.	8 × 21 in.	3	—
V.1 (1924) American	2,620 tons	hp 6,700* hp 2,400† = 18*/11† knots	1 × 5 in.	6 × 21 in.	—	—
V.4 (1927) American	4,080 tons	hp 3,175* hp 2,400† = 15*/8† knots	2 × 6 in.	4 × 21 in.	—	80
V.5 (1929) American	4,050 tons	hp 5,450* hp 2,540† = 17*/8† knots	2 × 6 in.	6 × 21 in.	—	—

The British gunboat *Redwing* (1881) in action

SLOOPS

Sloops and gunboats

After the widespread introduction of steam propulsion in the last decades of the 19th century, smaller warships came to be termed sloops and gunboats. Although the terminology was rather loose, generally speaking both sloops and gunboats were wooden vessels, under a thousand tons in displacement, which — owing to their limited coal-storage capacity — continued to carry a full rig of sails long after larger combatant vessels had abandoned rigging entirely. Most often, these light vessels were dispatched on the symbolic mission of 'showing the flag,' that is, of making some smaller nation aware of the possibility of military intervention. Historians have called this policy 'gunboat diplomacy.' Many European powers, as well as America, practiced it.

The earliest gunboats carried, on a flush maindeck, slide-mounted guns that could be shifted to either side for combat. Later gunboats, like sloops, had a fo'c'sle and poop decks and still carried the heavier guns on traversing slides. They housed lighter cannon at broadside gunports. They generally had a three-masted fore-and-aft rig with the funnel stepped between, the foremast and mainmast. Originally steered from the poop deck, they gradually adopted a bridge sited forward of the funnel.

In the 1860's and 1870's sloops and gunboats gradually passed from wood to steel construction. They carried breech-loading guns on central pivot mountings on the broadside, generally with two on the fo'c'sle, two or four in the waist and two on the poop. Until 1900 they were built in large numbers as instruments of colonial expansion, but after the turn of the century severe reductions were made. As naval rivalry increased, there was a natural reluctance to spend money on vessels of little combatant value. In addition, the introduction of radio permitted faster communication and a more centralized control over naval units, diminishing the need for far-flung, independently operating sloops and gunboats. By 1914 these vessels were generally considered obsolete.

World War I, however, amply demonstrated that even total war had many side-shows in which sloops and gunboats could be effective. By 1916 the submarine threat to mercantile ship-

Profile of *Redwing*

(*Above*) The German gunboat *Iltis* (1898). (*Below*) The British sloop *Cadmus* (1904).

ping had re-established the sloop as a convoy escort. The vessel also proved itself invaluable for minesweeping.

The *Flower*-class sloop

Late in 1914 the pressing need for minesweepers induced the British Admiralty to order a dozen shallow draft vessels. To speed construction, the design was made simple; it conformed largely with mercantile designs, so that the orders could be placed with commercial shipyards that did not specialize in naval work. The result was the *Flower*-class sloop, which proved versatile and reliable. By the end of the war over one hundred of them had been built for the British and French navies. Although initially intended for coastal minesweeping, they were mainly employed in anti-submarine and patrol work. They displayed fine seaworthiness on the oceans.

With a strong vertical stem (strengthened for ramming), a fo'c'sle and two slim funnels, these handsome vessels were powered by reciprocating (piston) engines turning a single screw for a speed of 16 knots. The armament comprised two 12-pounder guns, altered to 4-inch or 4.7-inch guns in later units, and—bearing in mind the vessels were designed as minesweepers—the magazine was placed aft. Some units were modified to resemble merchant ships (Q-ships) and had their armament concealed behind lidded ports.

The sloop between the wars

Although seldom so-classed, vessels with sloop characteristics continued to be built after World War 1 either as escorts or minesweepers—two very similar types which were, in fact, interchangeable. While practically all navies needed minesweepers, only those which had to maintain sea communications—and this invariably meant the navies of the colonial powers—built escort sloops.

The British built more sloops than other nations as she was heavily committed to protecting overseas trade. The new vessels had turbine propulsion and shallower draft. In 1930, the first London Naval Treaty defined a sloop as a vessel not exceeding (a) a displacement of 2,000 tons, (b) a speed of 20 knots and (c) an armament of four 6-inch guns and no torpedo tubes. Only the United States Navy built up to this limit—the sloops *Charleston* and *Erie*—but the French closely approached it with the 1,969-ton *Bougainville* class which made 15½ knots on diesel engines, were armed with three 5.5-inch

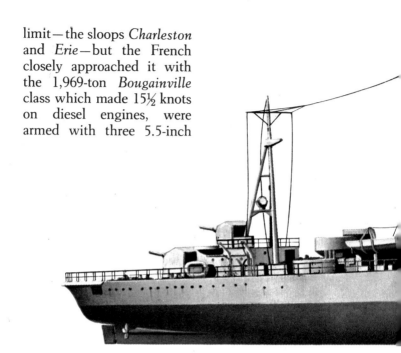

guns, fitted for minelaying, and carried an aircraft.

By the outbreak of World War II, the British ocean escort sloop had advanced to a vessel of 1,250 tons, 19 knots and eight 4-inch

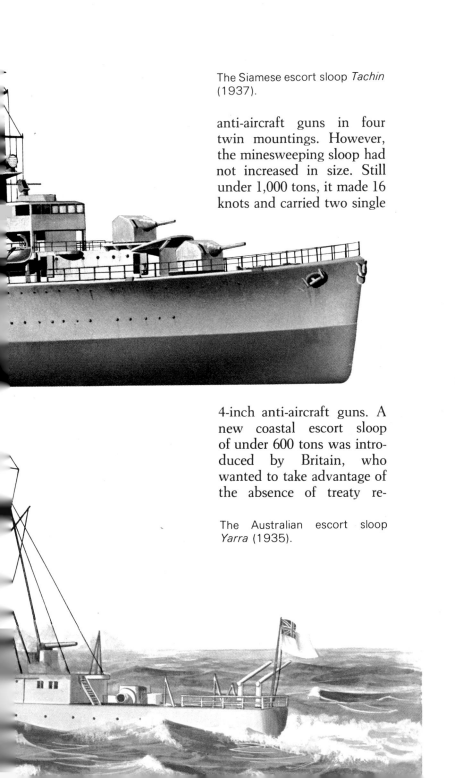

The Siamese escort sloop *Tachin* (1937).

anti-aircraft guns in four twin mountings. However, the minesweeping sloop had not increased in size. Still under 1,000 tons, it made 16 knots and carried two single

4-inch anti-aircraft guns. A new coastal escort sloop of under 600 tons was introduced by Britain, who wanted to take advantage of the absence of treaty re-

The Australian escort sloop *Yarra* (1935).

strictions on vessels under this tonnage. Making a speed of
20 knots, this little sloop mounted one 4-inch gun.

War construction

Even before the outbreak of World War II, the United States
and Britain realized they would face a critical shortage in escorts if Germany made war. Existing designs—good as they
were—were unsuitable for series production in the United
Kingdom. Therefore, drawing on its experience in World War
I, Britain sought a commercial prototype which would meet
minimum naval requirements. A private yard proposed a mod-
ification of the British whale-catcher *Southern Pride,* and this
was accepted. Large orders were again placed—as in World
War I—with yards that did not specialize in naval work, and
the vessels passed into service as *Flower*-class corvettes. Of
925 tons, they steamed at 16 knots with reciprocating machinery, and were armed with one 4-inch gun and anti-submarine equipment.

Although the corvette performed yeoman service, it proved
a little too small for ocean work and was replaced in 1942 by
the larger and faster twin-screw *River*-class frigates. So that
production could be speeded still further, the design of the

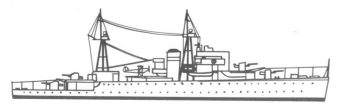

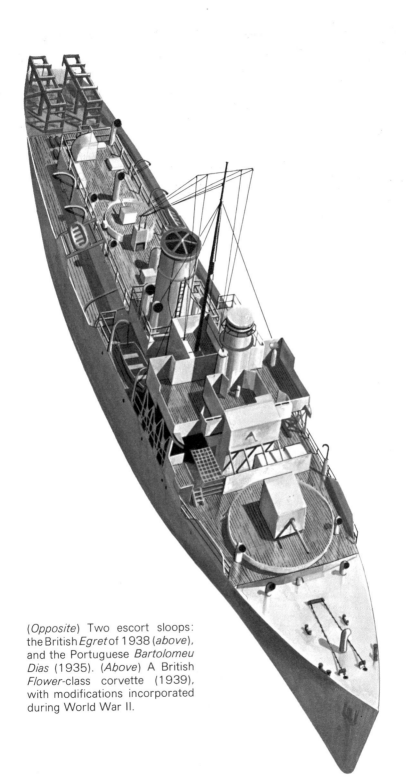

(*Opposite*) Two escort sloops:
the British *Egret* of 1938 (*above*),
and the Portuguese *Bartolomeu
Dias* (1935). (*Above*) A British
Flower-class corvette (1939),
with modifications incorporated
during World War II.

F108

frigate was slightly altered to suit prefabricated construction, and the vessels were completed as either anti-submarine (*Loch* class) or anti-aircraft (*Bay* class) escorts. The United States Navy produced a destroyer escort that was slightly larger and faster than the frigate. Japan had neglected escort vessels before the war and had hurriedly to embark on a war program. At first, her escorts were given only a fifth priority, after aircraft carriers, submarines, destroyers and minesweepers. But with American submarines taking a heavy toll of Japanese merchant shipping, escorts were advanced to fourth, and then second, priority during 1943–44. All except half the final series were diesel-engined vessels capable of 19½ knots and armed with two or three 4.7-inch guns. With the slightly smaller *Kaitoban*

F353

class, the odd-numbered vessels were diesel-engined for a speed of 16½ knots; turbines were installed in the even-numbered vessels because of a shortage of diesel machinery and proved a knot faster.

The modern frigate

At the end of World War II, a variety of small warships overstocked the navies of many nations. The frigate category had been produced widely, along with destroyer escorts and escort sloops. These vessels, to a greater or lesser degree, faced obsolescence.

The minesweeping sloop was phased out because technical advances had created mines far more sophisticated than the old, moored contact mines. Now there were mines that exploded in response to the vibrations propagated in the sea by a ship's machinery or to the magnetism of the steel in a ship's hull. The new minesweeper would have to be silent and nonmagnetic.

The destroyer also became obsolete as an attack ship. Although new destroyers were built, they were now fast anti-submarine and anti-aircraft escorts for the fleet.

(*Above*) The British frigate *Londonderry* (1961). (*Below*) The Danish frigate *Peder Skram* (1967), powered by gas turbines and diesel engines.

The wartime frigate was first threatened by the conventionally powered fast submarine and then completely outpaced by the nuclear submarine, so that a new type of frigate with destroyer speed was required. As an interim measure, until the new generation of fast frigates with sufficient speed to counter nuclear submarines was in service, many destroyers were converted to frigates. To keep size down, the first new units were built for specialized roles—for anti-submarine, anti-aircraft or aircraft-directing duties—and were intended to form self-supporting groups. But as the numbers that could be built were so restricted, this policy was later reversed and the general purpose frigate was introduced.

Frigates increased in size to accommodate a missile armament, more sophisticated weaponry and complex electronics (radar, communications, missile test equipment, etc.). They were given nuclear-powered propulsion by the United States Navy to accompany the nuclear-powered carrier *Enterprise*. The frigate became so complex and expensive that the pendulum started to swing the other way, and the tendency today is to revert to a frigate that is cheaper, easier and quicker to build.

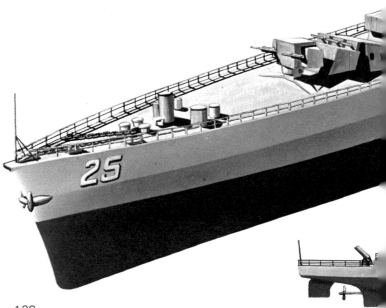

Two missile-armed frigates: (*above*) the American nuclear-powered *Bainbridge* (1962) and (*below*) the French *Suffren* (1966).

The gas turbine proved helpful in this respect. Thus, in 1968, the British Navy placed in service the first all-gas turbine frigate, the *Exmouth*.

In recent years, Britain settled exclusively on gas-turbine propulsion for frigates, bypassing the combined diesel and gas propulsion systems fitted by other nations. In fact, the British envisage two types of modern frigates to meet their defense requirements today: a sophisticated frigate armed with a long-range missile system and matching radar, and a simpler class with a short-range missile system that does not require elaborate radar.

The United States has continued to fit its escort vessels with steam turbines. But its next series (for which design details had yet to be fully settled at the time of this writing) will probably incorporate gas turbines.

The modern corvette

A small, basically simple vessel, well able to cope with conventional warfare and generally lighter than 1,000 tons, has been developed in several navies in recent years. Termed a corvette, this craft is usually diesel-propelled. With active fin-

stabilization ('power-steering'), it can operate effectively in rough weather. Its development was spurred by the emergence of new nations which lacked the technical experience and trained personnel to include the most advanced frigates in their navies, as well as by the worldwide need for policing craft fit for use in minor disturbances where sophisticated weaponry would be out of place. An example of the latter instance came during the confrontation between Indonesia and Malaysia in the early 1960's. At that time, Britain sent ships to keep peace in the area. These vessels were specially fitted with manually operated 20-millimeter guns, despite the fact that they were already armed with missiles and fully automatic guns.

Modern Soviet escort vessels generally fall into this last category. On a limited displacement, they cannot incorporate advanced electronic anti-submarine detection or weapons systems, nor can they endure prolonged ocean-going service.

If the cycle of warship development that began with gunboats and sloops has now come full circle in today's frigates and corvettes, then it would seem that old design concepts are still valid in the modern world — at least in the case of performing missions related to conventional warfare.

Corvettes: (*above*) the Italian *Albatros* (1955) and (*below*) the Ghanaian *Keta* (1966); both are diesel-engined vessels.

MISCELLANEOUS VESSELS

From time to time in the evolution of the warship, there appeared unconventional craft. Some influenced the mainstream of warship design, while others proved unique dead ends. A number of these interesting vessels are described below.

Russia's circular ironclad

Designed by the Russian Navy to protect the mouth of the River Dnieper, this Black Sea fleet vessel was made circular to provide a very large displacement on a shallow draft. The prototype, *Novgorod,* had a flat-bottomed hull with a diameter of 101 feet, a draft of 13¼ feet and a displacement of 2,491 tons. Although the freeboard at the side was only 1¾ feet, the deck was arched slightly, and was 5 feet above the waterline at the center, where there was a thickly armored circular barbette that contained two slide-mounted, 11-inch, breech-loading guns. The ship was protected by an armored belt and an armored deck.

On trials the *Novgorod* attained about 8 knots. She proved unmanageable in a river while going with the current, but behaved better when stemming the current or in open calm water. Russia's circular ironclads proved a failure as floating fortresses. Among other things, they demonstrated that there was no alternative to shipshape form for maneuverable sea-going vessels.

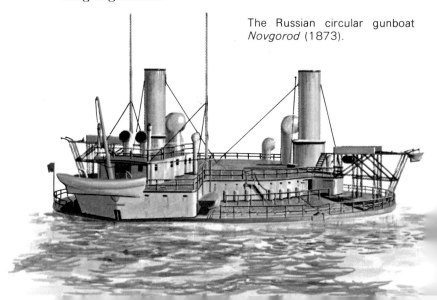

The Russian circular gunboat *Novgorod* (1873).

The British ram *Polyphemus* (1882).

The British torpedo ram *Polyphemus*

The *Polyphemus* was first conceived with the ram as her only weapon. However, the design was later modified to incorporate submerged torpedo tubes and a few quick-firing guns.

The hull was cylindrical with the curve slightly flattened above water and brought to a point at the keel; the ends were also brought to a point. With a displacement of 2,640 tons, she had dimensions of 240 feet × 40 feet × 20 feet with only 4½ feet of freeboard amidships. The hull was protected by 3-inch plate carried to a depth of 6 feet below the waterline, and the conning tower and casings for the funnel and ventilators were similarly armored. There was a light casing on the foredeck, which extended back to the conning tower and supported the wheelhouse and chartroom, and a hurricane deck for stowing boats. A speed of 17 knots was realized on a total output of 5,500 horsepower.

Only one vessel similar to the *Polyphemus* was ever built, and that was the American ram *Katahdin* (ex-*Ammen*) some 15 years later, but neither ever found general acceptance.

The British river gunboat

During the period of British colonial expansion, increasing support was given to the army in the field by naval units making the widest possible use of rivers. Although small warships could navigate the mouths and lower reaches of most rivers, special craft were required for the shallower upper reaches.

Only a flat bottom could provide the necessary shallow draft. Thus, the earliest river gunboats were like powered pontoons,

(*Above*) British river gunboat *Ladybird* (1916). (*Below*) The British bombardment monitor *Abercrombie* (1915).

with crew space and machinery on deck and light guns on the superstructure. But, during World War I, Britain built 24 river gunboats for service in the Middle East. Twelve vessels were of the large *Insect* class, displacing 645 tons. The *Insect* gunboat was about 240 feet in overall length, 36 feet across, and 8½ feet in depth, with a draft of 4 feet that left some 4½ feet of freeboard. These boats were armed with two 6-inch and two 12-pounder guns.

The British bombardment monitor

In their advance through Belgium in 1914, the Germans extended their western flank to the coast of Europe. Hence, the British Navy was called upon to assume a traditional shore-bombardment role along the European coast in support of Allied land armies. Four spare twin 14-inch gun turrets were used in a new type of shore bombardment vessel inaptly classed as a monitor.

As shallow draft was essential, the hull could not be made deep, and the turret and barbette therefore projected conspicuously above the upper deck. Abaft the turret was a small bridge structure with the fire control equipment carried at the head of a tall tripod mast used for long-range spotting. Although armor was applied to the turret and barbette, and

144

armored bulkheads were provided fore and aft, the side was left unprotected except for a deep anti-torpedo bulge.

Even before they were completed, the usefulness of the 14-inch gun monitors was very evident and, when four twin 15-inch turrets were made available, four other units were rushed to completion. Further monitor classes, armed with guns from old battleships and cruisers, were later built.

National coast defense ships

In the pre-*Dreadnought* era, minor navies built battleships smaller than those possessed by great maritime powers, principally on the grounds of cost. But another reason was that their craft were intended solely for coastal defense and could therefore sacrifice speed and radius. However, after the *Dreadnought* (see page 20), little cost could be saved with small coastal ships, and the type became obsolete.

Only three groups of coast defense ships were completed after the *Dreadnought*: the Swedish *Sverige* class, Finnish *Väinämöinen* class and Siamese *Dhonburi* class.

The Swedish vessels were fast, well-protected and a worthy match for the German armored ship *Deutschland*, which was so widely acclaimed a few years later. The Finnish

ships were a remarkable combination of size and power, had a well-disposed secondary dual-purpose battery, and adopted diesel-electric propulsion. The tonnage limitation on the Siamese ships was too severe for them to compare favorably. They were rather short for the weights carried but, with diesel engines, had a good radius of action.

The Swedish multi-purpose ship *Gotland*

This vessel was completed in 1934 as a replacement for the cruiser *Fylgia* (1907) and the minelayer *Klas Fleming* (1914), and, as she was also fitted to operate 11 aircraft, the *Gotland* was one of the most versatile warships ever built.

The flush-decked hull was protected by a deep belt and an armored deck. The main guns were carried in two twin

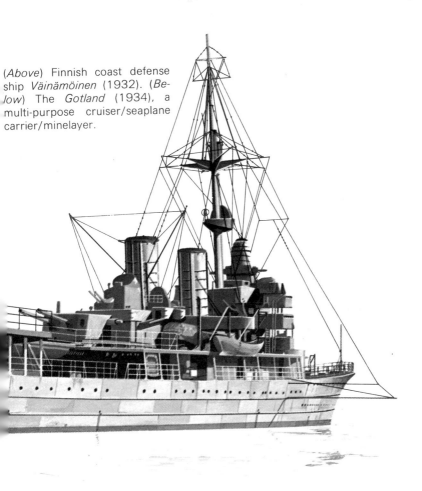

(*Above*) Finnish coast defense ship *Väinämöinen* (1932). (*Below*) The *Gotland* (1934), a multi-purpose cruiser/seaplane carrier/minelayer.

turrets and two single casements on each side of the bridge, while mines were stowed on the main deck and laid through stern ports. Aircraft were stowed on the flight deck aft. By a system of rails they were moved forward to the training catapult from which they could be launched at two-minute intervals. At an overall length of 443 feet, a width of 50¼ feet and a depth of 16½ feet, the *Gotland* had a standard displacement of 4,750 tons and attained a speed of 27½ knots with a two-shaft geared turbine installation of 33,000 hp.

The fast minelayer

Despite the importance of minelaying, few ships are ever built specifically for this role. Therefore, two surprising

features of Britain's 1938–39 naval program were the allocations for four minelayers—the *Abdiel* class—and the high speed with which they were endowed.

On a displacement of 2,650 tons these vessels had an overall length of 418 feet and were flush-decked with the greater part of the main deck aft used to stow 160 mines. They were powered by two sets of geared turbines developing 72,000 hp for a speed of 39 knots. They were armed with 4.7-inch guns in twin mountings fore and aft, controlled by a director on the bridge; this armament proved sufficient to ward off attacks by destroyers, the only vessels fast enough to challenge them.

The Japanese torpedo cruisers *Oi* and *Kitakami*

In 1933 the Imperial Japanese Navy introduced a new oxygen-fueled 24-inch torpedo (the 'Long Lance') which had a range of 43,500 yards at 36 knots and a 1,100-pound warhead. This weapon, which completely outclassed the standard 21-inch torpedo in other navies, was fitted to all new cruisers and destroyers under construction, and to many earlier cruisers and destroyers.

Two light cruisers, the *Oi* and *Kitakami,* were completely rearmed in 1941. They were fitted with five quintuple banks of 24-inch torpedo tubes on each side amidships; the sides were sponsoned out to provide the appropriate training arcs. No other warship ever equalled the torpedo armament carried by these two vessels. The gun armament was reduced to four 5.5-inch guns. Later 5-inch anti-aircraft weapons in twin mountings fore and aft were fitted. At that time the light anti-aircraft armament was considerably reinforced to comprise thirty-six 25-millimeter guns in six triple shields and 18 single gun stations.

Combatant naval auxiliaries

All navies have drawn on their mercantile marines during hostilities to supplement the ships and personnel of the fighting fleets; but the combatant value of naval auxiliaries has diminished as warships become more sophisticated. In World War II, the conversion to aircraft carriers and anti-aircraft vessels provided the most combatant auxiliary vessels.

The former cross-channel passenger ferry *Ulster Queen* was extensively altered to ship an anti-aircraft armament of six 4-inch guns in three twin mountings, eight 2-pounders in two quadruple mountings and ten single 20-millimeter guns; she was provided with a high-angle director aft, air warning radar at the mastheads and surface warning radar on the bridge.

But the most significant conversions were undertaken by the Imperial Japanese Navy, which turned seven passenger liners into aircraft carriers. Although these vessels lacked the speed and protection of the full fleet carriers, they nevertheless were valuable additions to attack groups.

(*Opposite*) The Japanese torpedo cruiser *Kitakami*, converted in 1941. (*Below*) The British minelayer *Abdiel* (1941).

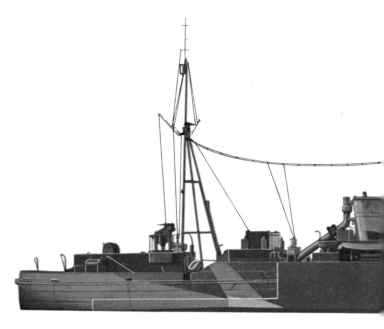

The paddle aircraft carrier

Early in World War II, the United States became highly pressed for training carriers for its expanding naval flight program. The vessels were converted from two excursion paddle steamers and commissioned as the *Wolverine* and *Sable* in 1942–43. Their superstructures were dismantled and a flight deck, overhanging the bow and stern, was built over the existing hull. As hangars were not provided, the flight deck was close to the waterline, and aircraft landed and took off with the minimum interval.

(*Above*) The British auxiliary anti-aircraft ship *Ulster Queen*, converted in 1941. (*Below*) The American training carrier *Wolverine*, which was converted in 1942, with side-paddle propulsion.

The British tank landing craft

After Nazi Germany's conquest of Europe in 1940, the British realized that the continent would eventually be liberated only by a massive assault from the sea. Thus, special craft would be required to land the heavy equipment used by modern armies in the field. Because of the narrowness of the English Channel, the craft did not need to be particularly seaworthy. The basic requirements were simple design for rapid production, the ability to beach in order to put men and vehicles ashore (meaning a shallow draft) and a bow-ramp that could be raised and lowered to ease the loading and off-loading of men and material.

The resulting landing craft for men and vehicles resembled one another, except that the latter type was larger. The British tank landing craft Mark I was designed to carry three 40-ton tanks. The capacity of the tank-deck determined the dimensions: 151¼ feet in overall length; 29 feet wide; a 3-foot draft forward and 5¾ feet aft. Since the bow-ramp needed to be bluff, the possibility of high speed was eliminated. However, two diesel engines, totaling 1,000 hp, gave 10 knots. The bridge, crew space and machinery were crowded aft. A purely defensive armament of two light anti-aircraft guns was mounted in the bridge wings.

The American landing ship tank (LST)

Although Britain's landing craft performed well enough in limited operations, they had been designed neither for seaworthiness nor heavy loads. After Pearl Harbor, the United States found itself forced to fight across many thousands of miles of ocean to carry the war to the enemy, particularly in the Pacific. United States planners set about producing new generations of landing ships that were to revolutionize the role of seapower in invasion forces.

Since the shallow draft needed for beaching a landing craft is incompatible with the deep draft required for seaworthiness, the United States Navy was pressed to the limits of ingenuity to create an ocean-going landing ship. Ballast tanks yielded the answer, however. By pumping seawater into the tanks, the flat-bottomed hull could be weighted down, making it sink deeper into the water. By pumping the ballast out at the time of an amphibious operation, the tank deck and flat hull were brought almost even with the waterline for beaching. The Mark II LST carried as many as 30 heavy tanks and other vehicles.

(*Above*) British tank landing craft *Mk.8* (1945). (*Below*) An American landing ship tank of the *County* class (1953).

The American landing ship dock (LSD)

In the first waves of an amphibious assault, swifter, more maneuverable tank landing craft—perhaps carrying only one or two tanks or other armored vehicles—went ashore. The LST Mark II usually beached and off-loaded its huge stores of motorized equipment only after the beachhead was comparatively secure. Thus, a mother ship was needed to serve as a berth for the smaller landing craft, to transport them fully loaded to the scene of operations and launch them.

For a time, the Mark II LST played the role. But then the much larger landing ship dock came out of shipyards. With an overall length of 457¾ feet, the LSD was 130 feet longer than the LST. Its displacement of 4,200 tons dwarfed the LST's 1,625-ton displacement. The LSD's stern-ramp structure was really a system of locks and docks, permitting the big ship to take into itself smaller craft and put them underway again later. Like the Mark II LST, the landing ship dock was equipped with ballast tanks and pumps that allowed it to change its draft. The LST and the LSD together revolutionized amphibious warfare.

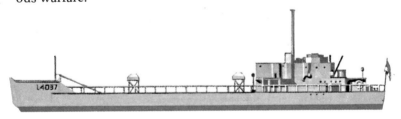

(*Above*) American landing ship dock, *Thomaston* class (1955). (*Below*) British headquarters ship *Bulolo,* converted in 1942.

The headquarters ship

In large-scale combined operations during World War II, a prime requirement was the provision of a headquarters ship from which the naval and military commanders could correlate the activities of their widely dispersed units ashore and afloat.

In order not to tie up a major naval unit in such a restrictive role, it was found expedient to equip medium-sized merchant ships with a good turn of speed because they had the necessary space for fitting the wide range of communications equipment required and for accommodating the naval and military staffs. A typical example was the former Australian passenger vessel *Bulolo,* which was first requisitioned by the British Navy in 1940 as an armed merchant cruiser. In 1942 she was converted to a headquarters ship and served at the Sicilian, Italian and Normandy landings. She displaced 9,111 tons and was powered by diesel engines of 6,000 hp at a speed of 15 knots. Her defensive armament included four 4-inch anti-aircraft guns in two twin mountings, five single 40-millimeter anti-aircraft guns and fourteen single 20-millimeter anti-aircraft guns. She could carry 238 troops and under her davits housed six personnel landing craft for putting them ashore.

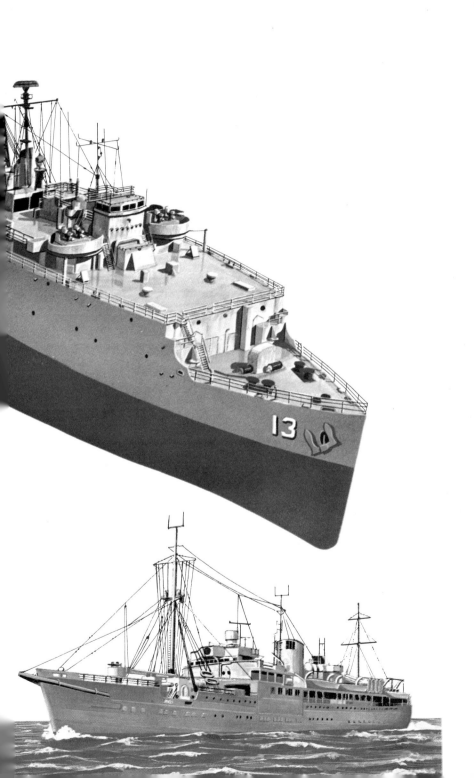

BOOKS TO READ

Jane's Fighting Ships, a yearbook that has been published annually since 1898 by Jane's Yearbooks, London, England. The coverage of the world's warships is expert, up-to-date, and heavily detailed.

Weyer's Warships of the World. G. Albrecht. The United States Naval Institute, Annapolis, Maryland, and the *Dictionary of American Fighting Ships,* U.S. Government Printing Office, Washington, D.C.

History of United States Naval Operations in World War II. Samuel Eliot Morison. Little, Brown, 1959; 13 volumes.

Aircraft Carriers. N. Polmar. Doubleday; current revised edition.

The Atomic Submarine and Admiral Rickover. Clay Blair. Holt, 1954.

Nautilus 90 North. Commander William R. Anderson, U.S.N. World, 1959.

The Battle of Midway. Irving Werstein. Crowell, 1961.

D-Day the Sixth of June 1944. D.A. Howarth. McGraw-Hill, 1959.

Mr. Lincoln's Admirals. C.E.N. Macartney. Funk & Wagnall, 1956.

The Ancient Mariners: seafarers and seafighters of the Mediterranean in ancient times. Lionel Casson. Macmillan, 1959.

GLOSSARY

ABAFT: In back of; toward the stern.

AMIDSHIPS: At the middle or center of the ship.

ATHWARTSHIPS: Running across the width, or beam, of the ship.

AXIAL: Along the centerline or axis; hence, axial fire is across the stem or the stern.

BORE: The hollow gun barrel; the diameter of the bore is usually measured in hundredths of an inch, or in millimeters.

BOW: The front part of the ship.

BULKHEAD: Bulkheads are watertight walls or partitions used to divide the ship into compartments.

CALIBER: This term has several usages. The most common is with respect to the inside diameter of the bore of the gun, in hundreths of an inch. Hence, a 30-caliber weapon has a bore diameter of 30/100ths of an inch. With respect to larger ordnance, caliber often is used as measure of the gun's length—specifically, the combined length of the shell-chamber and the bore. Caliber then gives the gun's length as a multiple of its bore diameter. Thus, a 50-caliber, 6-inch gun would be 25 feet long.

CASEMATE: An armored enclosure for a gun or guns.

DISPLACEMENT: The weight of the volume of water that is displaced by the ship's hull. Ships are rated with a standard displacement and a full-load displacement.

DRAFT: The depth to which the hull must be submersed in order to displace a volume of water sufficient to keep the ship afloat.

FO'C'SLE (FORECASTLE): The forecastle was the upper deck in the bow of sailing ships. Below it were the main deck and the lower deck.

FREEBOARD: The height of the ship's side between the waterline and the main deck or gunwale; the hull above the waterline.

GUNWALE (GUNNEL): The upper edge of the ship's side.

HOLD: The interior of the ship beneath the main or lower deck.

HULL: The ship's body, comprising the sides, the stem, the stern and the bottom.

KEEL: The spine of the hull running axially along the bottom.

PORT: An opening, as for a gun; to port, to the left of the bow.

POOP DECK: The raised deck at the stern of sailing vessels.

RIFLING: As opposed to the smooth bore, the modern rifled bore is grooved in such a way as to impart spin to the projectile.

RIGGING: The arrangement of the sailing ship's masts, sails, ropes, etc.

SHELL: Shell is loaded into the chamber at the breech as opposed to through the muzzle. It can be either a single unit including both projectile and a casing containing the propellant, or—in the largest guns—can be loaded separate from the propellant, contained in bags.

SHOT: The classic cannonball, muzzle-loaded, round and solid, with the propellant loaded separately.

STARBOARD: To the right of the bow.

INDEX

SOON TO BE PUBLISHED